I Will
if
You Will

Sandra ~

Blessings to you!

[signature]

I Will
if
You Will

Maxie L. Hellmann

PUBLISHING

Cover design by Joe Potter Designs
On the web: www.joepotter.com

Published by Spiritfire Publishing, LLC
www.spiritfirepublishing.com

Spiritfire Publishing is committed to publishing works inspired by the Holy Spirit for the purpose of sharing the Father's love by bringing the message of Jesus Christ and the Gospel of the Kingdom to all nations. The company's foundational Scriptures are Matthew 3:11–12, Mark 16:15–20, Acts 1:8, Acts 2:2–4, and 1 Thessalonians 5:19.

The opinions of the author are not necessarily the same as those of Spiritfire Publishing, LLC.

ISBN: 978-0-9972078-0-4 (Paperback)
ISBN: 978-0-9972078-6-6 (Hardcover)
REL006140: Religion / Biblical / Prophecy

This Book Is Dedicated To My Grandchildren

Elijah Thomas
Madelyn Christina
Juliet Anne
Elianna Mae
Judah Rhodes
Finlin Zachary
Sawyer Thomas
Messer Lyric
Willamina Paisley

May you each not only grow up to be amazing men and women of God,
but I pray each one of you will be a radical Jesus-lover as children,
so full of the Word of God and Holy Spirit that you touch lives
everywhere you go.
Full of faith, always praying,
Never fearing, always standing.

I pray the Lord's protection and provision over each of you
and that God's blessings will flow to you from
the North, the South, the East, and the West.

Each one of you holds a very special place in my heart,
and I thank God daily for the blessings you are to me.

I pray God will use this book to make the world a better place
for you all to grow up in.

Acknowledgments

First of all, I want to thank my Lord and Savior, Jesus
Christ.
Without Him none of this would be possible.
I commit this book to You, Lord!

———•—◆—•———

My husband, John
Who is always there for me.
Thank you for always encouraging, uplifting,
and believing in me.
Making sure I have all I could possibly need
Most importantly, keeping me covered in prayer.
May God pour out His blessings on you for being
the best husband ever!

———•—◆—•———

My daughter, Candi
Who has encouraged me at every turn,
edited this entire book,
and prayed for me and this project incessantly.
Thank you for loving me unconditionally
and making many sacrifices to see this to fruition.
May the Lord bless your every breath!

———•—◆—•———

My Prayer Warriors
Thank you for your faithfulness to pray for us
in every situation.
May the Lord bless each one of you abundantly!

———◆•◗•◆———

Family and Friends
Thank you for listening, praying, and always loving.
May God supply your every need!

———◆•◗•◆———

Friends on Dauphin Island
where most of this book was written.
Thank you for your prayers,
and for loving us, keeping us well fed, and still giving
me space while I wrote for weeks at a time.
You are all awesome!

———◆•◗•◆———

I love you all so much!

Table of Contents

Foreword

It is such an honor for me to be asked to write an introduction to this book by Maxie Hellmann. She and John have been a source of incredible blessing and spiritual life to our congregation for several years now, and she is recognized as a credible prophetic voice in our family of Believers.

I can give my whole-hearted support to this project for at least four reasons:

1. **I know Maxie.** Her humility and integrity are exemplary; I have observed her in moments of triumph, and in moments of difficulty. She and John remain as steady as a rock. Jesus said we would be known by our fruits, and her fruit is clearly Spirit-produced. This woman definitely loves Jesus!

2. **I agree with the message the Lord gave her for this nation.** It is not a popular message. It is not casually delivered, and it is not easily received. It is the sort of message delivered by Jeremiah. It is the rare teaching that judgment and mercy can go together. I am a fourth generation Pentecostal and believe we should celebrate the Spirit-Filled life, yet I am deeply troubled by the message of unequivocal prosperity and comfort that is embraced by so many in our branch of Christianity. It seems we have forgotten that Jesus died to deal with our sin problem, not to raise our level of comfort. In our arrogance we often select the scriptures we want to claim as though we're moving through a cafeteria line, choosing only what appeals to our appetite. We casually disregard the whole counsel of God, and the result is damaging imbalance. Jesus did promise an abundant life, but He also guaranteed that in this life we would have tribulation.

3. **I believe her warning is a strong message of hope.** Biblical hope is an extraordinary virtue. In Scripture it is placed alongside faith and love as one of three great qualities. But

hope has been replaced by optimism. Optimism does not always reflect reality; in fact it may at times deny reality. But hope recognizes the victory of Christ even in the presence of great trial. A look at the Biblical concept of hope recognizes the ultimate victory even though circumstances seem negative. Maxie understands that every rebuke is His mercy; every "thou shalt not" is really an "I love you." In understanding this balance we will experience the greatest hour in the history of the Church.

4. **I believe God has been vindicating Maxie and her message, and I believe He will continue to do so.** Her message has been confirmation to the message of our church since 2008. We are not privy to the details of His plan, and we don't always understand His timing, but we thank God for the Spirit among us, preparing our hearts for a future only He can see. We have a saying around here, "It ain't over till the fat angel sings!"

My recommendation is three-fold:

1. Read this book prayerfully and carefully, allowing the Holy Spirit to impart life to you.

2. Obey the message, and live with your eyes and ears fully open.

3. Share the message that Christ is victor, and His Church will always win the victory!

"Now to Him who is able to do far more abundantly beyond all that we ask or think, according to the power that works within us, to Him *be* the glory in the church and in Christ Jesus to all generations forever and ever. Amen."

- Ephesians 3:20-21 NASB

Stephen Chitty
Lead Pastor
Christian Life Church
Columbia, South Carolina

Preface

In my first book, *From Our Wicked Ways*, I discussed how "Many people wonder if God still speaks. God wonders if people still listen." In *I Will If You Will*, there are, once again, many references to hearing the voice of God.

I realize there are those who believe the only way God speaks to us today is through His written word, the Bible. There was a time I would have agreed, but about 20 years ago I began to wake up in the middle of the night and knew it was God who had awakened me. It wasn't an audible voice, but a still small voice, like the Bible speaks of in 1 Kings 19:12. I was just as certain the first time I heard that voice as I am today that it is the voice of God.

God certainly speaks to us through the Bible. He also speaks to us through dreams, visions, and other ways. We must not limit God in how He speaks to His children. After all, I would say that God Almighty can speak to us any way He chooses, wouldn't you?

After the first time I recognized His voice in the night, I realized God had been speaking to me for most of my life. I just hadn't understood that it was Him. He began giving me dreams and even visions when I was a small child. He also led me to read certain parts of scripture as He would speak to me. I believe at times I thought that still small voice was possibly my own thoughts. Other times, I pushed it away because it wasn't what I wanted to hear. After recognizing His voice that first time, I have refused to deny that I hear Him speak to me, although some have tried to discourage me.

I also want to make it clear that I do not take hearing the voice of God lightly. It is one of the biggest blessings in my life. Honestly, I don't know how I could live without Him speaking to me now that I know His voice.

I could not possibly count the number of people who have asked me, "But how do you *hear* God?" That is a very hard question to answer. I can give you clues, but truly you must hear God for yourself.

There is one thing God will never do and that is to tell you something which contradicts the Bible. If you hear a voice that is telling you something which does not line up with the Word of God, that is *not* the voice of the Lord.

One other thing I want to talk to you about is what to do when someone gives you a word from the Lord. The Bible tells us we must test the spirits. Read 1 John 4:1-3.

Take the words you read in this book to the Lord in prayer. Ask Him how or if they apply to you. What does He want you to do with what you have read or heard? You need to do that every time someone tells you a word is from God. If you don't feel that word applies to you in any way, put it on the shelf and read it again at a later time. Just make sure you are prepared in your heart to act on those words from the Lord, should He want you to.

One thing I recommend is to get your Bible and a journal or pen and paper, and get alone with the Lord. Leave your cell phone in the other room and turn off everything that distracts you. If you need to get up in the middle of the night to find some quiet time with God, then do so. I guarantee it will be worth the sleep you lose.

Now the Lord said to Abram,
"Go forth from your country,
and from your relatives and
from your father's house,
to the land which I will show you;
^{2}And I will make you a great nation,
and I will bless you,
and make your name great;
and so you shall be a blessing;
^{3}And I will bless those who bless you,
and the one who curses you I will curse.
And in you all the families of the earth
Will be blessed."

Genesis 12:1-3 (NASB)

I Will *if* You Will...

Our Walk of Faith

Let's begin in 2007, although I'm sure this walk actually started many years before. God has been preparing my husband and me for the journey we are on for a long, long time; however, that will have to be another book.

John and I both had full time jobs that we enjoyed. I had been employed, first with the County and then the City, for more than 12 years. I transported senior citizens around the city, sometimes driving 100-150 miles a day. Around 6am, I climbed into my work van and started my route. Most days it was pretty much the same, but this consistency created an environment that fostered endearing relationships with these people. We were very close, and some who rode my route for nearly a decade could only be described as family. When they were sick, I prayed for them. In the good times, we all laughed together. I watched as a number of those precious people went on to be with Jesus. Some I led to the Lord, but many were strong believers before I ever met them.

A typical workday for me began at 4am. When the alarm went off, I immediately got up. I'm not one of those "snooze-button" kind of people. After getting ready for work and eating breakfast, I always sat down for a little while with the Lord before leaving the house.

On Thursdays my day started earlier. That was the day I arrived at work around 5am. Walking through the parking lot, I prayed over every bus and van parked there. After going inside, I made sure chairs were set up in a little room where I led a prayer meeting with the bus drivers and then with the van drivers.

These prayer meetings were not my idea. God had spoken to me about starting a prayer meeting at work about a year earlier. I couldn't imagine any of my co-workers being interested in coming to a prayer meeting before or after work. When you start your day as early as we did, no one wanted to get to work even earlier, much less stay any later; and besides, they just didn't seem the type. I'm not sure what I thought "the type" was, but in my mind most of the people I worked with didn't fit that mold.

Wanting to be obedient to what I knew God had spoken to me, I kept an open mind to the idea and waited for Him to show me what, if anything, I was to do. It was a few months later when, during my morning prayer time, the Lord told me I was to talk to my director after work that very day about starting a prayer meeting. Whoa! I wasn't ready for this; however, I told God I would talk to her if she was in her office when I got off. Most days she was gone before I finished my route, so I didn't think too much about having to discuss this with her.

The Lord reminded me of what I needed to do as I drove into the parking lot that afternoon, and of course, my director was still there. Not expecting much, I went into her office. Briefly explaining that I would like to start a prayer meeting that would be held one morning a week before work, I was shocked at her response. She thought it was a great idea and would check downtown with the city manager. Less than 24 hours later the prayer meetings were given a green light.

> *We should never underestimate*
> *what God can do.*
> *If He has put something on your heart,*
> *do not be afraid to follow through with it.*
> *He will turn those mountains into pebbles*
> *that are easily kicked out of the way.*
> *How quickly we become discouraged,*

or even totally discount an idea,
because it doesn't seem
possible in the natural.
I believe God wants us to be
more expectant,
having faith that He will open doors
and pave the way before us.
When will we learn?
God isn't limited to the natural.
His capabilities are unlimited and
the supernatural is His domain.

Amazement is a good word for what took place in those prayer meetings. People attended from the very first day. They shared prayer requests, tears, and laughter. We came to know each other's hearts. My co-workers seemed to be drawn to that room. Some would come early, and others would slip in late, but come they did. What a blessing those times of prayer were to many people, especially me. I give God all the glory for what took place in that little room.

Although my job was secular, in many ways it felt like a ministry, and I loved it. There was no reason to leave my job. Our children were all grown up and out of the house. My work was a big part of my life, and it brought joy not only to those senior citizens who spent a good part of their day on my van, but to me as well.

However, one day in early May 2007, after pulling into the parking lot at the end of my shift, I had a strong sense that this season of my life was drawing to a close. There was paperwork to complete, a van to clean out, and other miscellaneous end-of-day duties; but concentrating on these tasks grew difficult, as the feeling grew stronger that I might not be there much longer. While driving to meet a friend after work, I got very serious with the Lord. If He was telling me something, I didn't want to miss it.

John was working second shift and I finally called him, desperately needing to share how I was feeling.

The first words out of his mouth were, "You go for it, Sweetie!"

I couldn't believe what I was hearing. My husband was always very reserved and took his time making decisions. His normal response would have been something like, "Well, we'll pray about it..."

I was committed to teaching a class for church that night so I tried to push this out of my mind in order to concentrate on the subject at hand. It was difficult. There was a part of me that felt a strange excitement creeping in.

Something was coming...something much bigger than anything I could imagine. I just knew it! And yet I didn't understand it at all.

Early the next morning I understood a little more. God awakened me before the alarm went off. He spoke to me so clearly. His presence was so powerful. The message He gave me couldn't have been more clear if it had literally been written on the wall.

You are to resign from your job.
Your last day will be the end of June.
As of July 1st, you won't be on
anyone's schedule but Mine.

There was no doubt in my mind that God had spoken this to me. My husband was in total agreement. We shared this with our pastor and he felt it was God as well. Three days later, I turned in my letter of resignation, giving five weeks notice. A season of my life was ending but, more importantly, a new season had begun.

The freedom I now felt was
sometimes overwhelming.
Sitting on the back porch swing,
looking out through the trees,
the tears would often
pour down my face.
The goodness of God was almost
more than I could bear.
I was thankful for so many things.
The wind in the trees,
every leaf rustling.
The sun shining through the

branches.
And the raindrops
hitting the deck above me.
I just couldn't get enough
of God's glory
and my back porch seemed to be
the best place to soak it in.

I didn't spend all my time sitting on the back porch swing. We must not go into neutral or park while we are waiting on the Lord to reveal His plan to us. There are ministry opportunities all around us, and time is far too short to waste. I stayed involved in my church, leading ladies' groups, mentoring, and helping my husband with a group that met in our home every week, in addition to offering my assistance as a chaplain in a nearby hospital.

I cannot stress enough how important it is that we don't just sit around waiting for God to open a door for us. We simply must continue to move forward. We must be willing to do whatever God puts in front of us as we watch His plan unfold for our lives.

It was more than four months before God shared part of His plan with me. On November 14th, 2007 at 1 am, I woke up to hear God say —

In January I am sending you to the churches.

Over the next few weeks He continued to show me what I was to do. On one of those nights, God gave me a word to take to the pastors in my city of Hickory, North Carolina. That word is just as applicable today as it was then.

Life as we know it is about to change.
If there is anything you need to repent of,
anything at all between you and God,
you need to take care of it. And call your
congregation to do the same.

Most of 2008 was spent meeting with pastors to give them the word from the Lord. I spoke to 83 pastors of all denominations face to face. The details of that journey and the response of each pastor can be found in my book *From Our Wicked Ways*.

As I look back on that year, I know God was preparing me for what was ahead. He was teaching me to trust Him with everything, to hear Him speak and just step out and do whatever He was telling me to. There was no room for being troubled over what others might think or even whether or not I was received well by the pastors or others God sent me to. He taught me to set my priorities and stand firm. Those priorities being —

1. Spend a lot of undistracted time with the Lord.
2. Listen for His voice.
3. Write down what He is saying.
4. Be swiftly obedient.

Speaking of being obedient, right now the Lord is telling me I need to talk about these four things a little more, so that's what we'll do.

A lot of time. Now just exactly how much time is a lot? Well, that depends on the person, the timing, and the situation. There are times in life where the best one can do is squeeze in a few minutes with the Lord while you are trying to soothe a crying baby, take a toddler to the potty, and help an older child with homework. And that little bit of time is certainly not undistracted.

God understands those times in a person's life, and He can speak peace into that parent or grandparent and say more in those few moments than others hear in an undisturbed hour.

This is, however, not the norm. Most of us spend way more time on our phones than we do with God, and when we do spend time praying, that phone is nearby and we grab it at every beep or ringtone.

So I will leave the amount of time you spend with the Lord between you and Him. You know when more time is needed with God, and you also know if you have allowed distractions to take over the majority of that time.

As for me, my best times with God seem to be in the middle of the night. The hard part is getting out of my warm bed to go sit somewhere to pray, but it's always worth it.

Next on the list is about listening for the voice of God. It would be impossible to count the times I have been asked the question, "But how do you HEAR God?"

The first thing I would say to that is God speaks to *all* of us, to everyone who will listen. He doesn't just have a chosen few that He talks to. Usually it will not be an audible voice. I have only heard God speak in an audible voice one time. It is more like a quiet voice that speaks to your spirit. I know, I know, some of you are saying that this isn't helping you understand how to hear God speak to you at all. I will say a bit more, but the bottom line is, you are going to have to spend time with Him and in His Word to get to know His voice.

One important thing we all need to remember is that God will never tell us anything that goes against scripture. If what you are hearing is contrary to the Bible, you are not hearing the voice of God.

Find a trusted friend or leader in your church who hears the voice of the Lord and begin to share what you are hearing from God. That person or persons should be able to help guide you along the way.

Ask God to help you hear and understand His voice. Share your heart with Him. Tell Him how much you want to not just talk *to* Him but *with* Him. He will be faithful to lead you into hearing clearly what He wants to tell you.

Third on the list is about writing down what God says to you. I believe this is very important. We think we will remember things, but very often we don't. Even if you aren't sure about what God is telling you, write it down anyway. Then you can go back and read those things over again at any time. I also recommend writing down the date, time, and sometimes the location when God speaks to you about something in particular. My God-journals are a huge blessing to me. I have been keeping journals since 1999. Before that I wrote on scraps of paper that ended up all over the place. (I still have a tendency to write down a word from the Lord on a scrap of paper or a napkin if my journal isn't handy. Just ask my family – they find them all over the place.)

And last, but certainly not least, is the part about being obedient. Not just obedient, but *swiftly* obedient. One definition of swift is to perform quickly or without delay. Now of course, it's a good idea to pray about what the Lord is telling you and also to share it with that trusted friend, but we often say we will pray about something God has told us to do, when in reality that is only an excuse to put off doing it. I know. I've been there. For years I asked the Lord numerous times a day to help me hear His voice clearly and to help me to be obedient immediately. I still ask Him for those things, just not as many times a day.

The Test

Early in 2009 my husband went to a staff meeting to find his job had been eliminated. While never doubting that the Lord had a plan, this news came as a blow to the momentum we were experiencing from our obedience to the task of the previous year. Relying solely on his income at this point, we quickly realized that we were being called to operate in an even greater faith.

That very evening, I sensed God was leading us to go to Waffle House. (Many of you will laugh, knowing how many Waffle House stories there are in my life.)

A short time later, John and I were sitting over coffee there, waiting to see what God had in store. We didn't have to wait long. Two ladies came in with two boys. I could tell in a glance that the boys were at the stage of eating their parents out of house and home. As they all sat down at the counter, God spoke to me.

You need to buy their dinner.

Immediately, I began to silently argue with Him.

"But God, John just lost his job. We don't even know when another paycheck will come in."

You need to buy their dinner.

"But God......."

By this time, John had watched this play out across my face and asked what was going on? I told him.

Of course he simply said, "Then we'd better do it."

In my mind I was still arguing. I even asked God if He realized how much those strapping young boys were probably going to eat.

By this time some of you are laughing.
But many are wondering how on earth
I can possibly argue with God like this;
and some are doubting
whether or not
a conversation of this sort
could even happen.

I don't believe there is any disrespect
when I argue with God.
He wants us to have a
relationship with Him,
not just be robots
that silently take orders.
Besides, He knows what's going
through our minds,
so we might just as well be truthful about it.

When our waitress stopped back by the table, I quietly asked her if she would give us their check. Immediately she wanted to know why. I told her God had spoken to us and we were supposed to buy their dinner. Totally unprepared for her reaction, I'm sure my mouth dropped open when she threw her hands up in the air, saying loudly, "Well, Hallelujah! Praise the Lord!"

Shortly she came back to us, asking if we wanted to tell them or could she? We told her she could tell them if she wanted to. She obviously wanted to...

The ladies looked over at us, the older one with eyes full of tears. When they came to our table to thank us, the older one said, "You have no idea what this means to us. You just have no idea."

We told them they were very welcome, and that God knew what they needed. It was He who deserved all the thanks.

We left shortly afterward, knowing our mission at Waffle House was completed. I have to admit that while being glad we had been obedient and that we could bless those people, somewhere in the back of my mind, I was still concerned about our money (or the lack thereof).

Upon arriving home, I went to see my neighbor, who is a good friend and prayer partner. I was going to share with her about John's job and ask for prayer that he would find another one quickly. She met me at the door, then said she would be right back and headed for the kitchen. She came back and put something into my hand, telling me she had been keeping this for the right time and that God had told her to give it to me. I hadn't even had a chance to tell her about the job yet, and I looked down to see a roll of money. $200 in twenty dollar bills! God was showing us very quickly that if we would only be obedient, He would take care of the rest.

The Call

Four days after my husband lost his job, I woke up with a horrendous headache. Not even able to pray, I just sat on my bed holding my Bible, saying, "Jesus, Jesus", while John went downstairs to get some toast and coffee for me.

All of a sudden, the presence of the Lord came into the room and I heard Him clearly say —

I want you to GO – and call My people to repentance.

I cannot say it was an audible voice. I have only heard God speak in an audible voice one time that I absolutely know of. This voice was so powerful, however, that everything in the room seemed to vibrate, even the pictures on the wall. I couldn't speak, only sit there holding my Bible, waiting...waiting...for what seemed like a long time, but I am sure it was only minutes, possibly seconds.

Then the presence of the Lord seemed to fade, and I realized my headache was completely gone! I ran downstairs to tell John what had happened and what God had spoken to me. After telling him what God had said, I saw he was waiting for the rest of it. But that was all.

*It is simply amazing how 11 words from God
can change everything.*

*We had known there was a divine plan for
us, but those words seemed to put flesh
and bone on a prophetic call that,
up until this moment,
existed solely as day-to-day
marching orders.
Still having no idea what this mandate would
look like, we set our faces toward the Lord.
Waiting...*

The Remnant

On April 8th, 2009, at 2:15am the Lord spoke this to me.

**I am looking for a remnant.
A remnant who will repent.
First of all, to cleanse their own hearts and
then, to cleanse their nation.**

Make no mistake, judgment is still coming, but it will not be nearly as severe if I can find a remnant who will repent for the sins of their nation. This nation must turn and turn quickly if there is to be any hope for survival.

A remnant, a remnant. So many people have asked me, "What exactly is a remnant?"

The definition I like best is from Webster's:

"A small portion; a slight trace; a fragment; a little bit; a scrap."

I recently read that Christians outnumber other religions in the United States by four to one. Out of all those people, is this really all God can get to sincerely intercede and repent for this nation? A remnant; a slight trace; a scrap...

We should be ashamed of ourselves. Are we, as people of God, too busy to commit to set aside a time to repent for the mess we Christians have helped to create? Do we really believe any election or the "right" politician will set this country on the path to greatness again?

Are we THAT deceived? Or possibly the deception is even greater. Possibly we are unable to see that our nation has become absolutely engulfed in sin. While many pastors have preached "Love and Grace, Love and Grace," because this is what makes people feel good, we cannot even recognize sin for what it is.

Yes! We have a loving God! And we would not even be here were it not for grace. But the Bible also teaches us about the repercussions of sin and the judgment that comes to a nation when that nation turns its back on Almighty God. We have become so desensitized to what sin really is that we don't even recognize it anymore. We allow, and even encourage, our children to watch things and be involved in activities that are abhorrent to God. People have actually said to me that they won't allow their kids to watch a movie if it has more than four curse words in it. *Four?* Is four a magic number? Does that make it okay if your children only hear four curse words in a movie instead of five, or ten?

We could write an entire book just on the detriment of television and movies, so we will move on. But I pray some of you are getting the point. A little sin in our lives gradually turns into a lot of sin. If we stray from the teachings of the Bible, we will eventually lose our way. And this is what has happened to our country. We have strayed too far, and have desperately lost our way. And it is possible that, as a nation, we may not ever find our way back...

If my people,
which are called by my name,
shall humble themselves,
and pray,
and seek
my face,
and turn from
their wicked ways;
then will I hear
from heaven,
and will forgive their sin,
and will
heal their land.

2 Chronicles 7:14 (KJV)

"heal our land"

It was May 5th, 2011, in the early morning hours, when I received more instruction from God on what we were to do. I woke up to a very evident presence of the Lord in the room. Usually I will get my Bible and journal and go into my office to pray when I wake up in the middle of the night. This time, God began to speak to me right away. I didn't have time to do anything except lay there in the dark and listen as He gave me detailed instructions of how we were to proceed. This was the first time God had used the word "missionaries" in regard to what John and I would be doing.

I understood God was calling us to full-time ministry, that we would be doing a lot of traveling, and the Holy Spirit would lead and direct us. I also knew the Lord was telling me we would be giving up most of our worldly possessions.

It all seemed so real to me. And no longer did it feel "in the future," but I sensed the timing was very near.

I have no idea how long the Lord spoke to me. It seemed like quite a while and He gave me a lot of information. At the end of this I had a vision. Very clearly, I saw the back of a motor home a few feet from the end of our bed. The lights were on and I could tell it was traveling down a road. Across the back it read *"heal our land"* in all lower case script lettering, glowing with a bright white light. For a short time, this vision was so clear I felt I could touch it. Then it began to fade.

Gathering up my Bible and journal, I walked down the hall toward my office, but didn't go inside as I normally would. I went just inside the door, stood quietly, and looked around. Then I did the same thing at each room as I made my way back up the hall. I remember feeling sort of strange as I did this. It felt almost surreal. It seemed as if it wasn't really me walking through that house. I have had people tell me I was actually saying goodbye to my home at that time, even though I didn't realize that's what I was doing.

As I stopped just inside the door of the living room, God spoke to me. His voice was so gentle, so loving. God knew this was not going to be easy for me.

Do you realize you are going to have to give most of this up?

"Yes, Lord." I replied, not truly having an idea of the sacrifice we would be making to answer this call on our lives.

When I am speaking to groups of people,
I often get emotional at this point.
It has nothing to do
with the things we have given up,
but rather the absolute
sweetness of the Lord
as He spoke to me that night.
"Do you realize you are going to have to
give most of this up?"
He knew my heart, knew I was willing,
but that I didn't really understand the cost.
Luke writes...

25 Great crowds were following
Jesus.
He turned around
and said to them,
26 "If you want to be My follower
you must love Me
more than your own father and mother,
wife and children, brothers and sisters---

yes,
more than your own life.
Otherwise, you cannot be My
disciple.
27 And you cannot be My disciple if
you do not carry your own cross
and follow Me.
28 But don't begin until you
count
the cost.
Luke 14:25-28a (NLT)

Jesus is telling us here
that if we are a true disciple of His,
we must be willing to give up
everything.
This is not only material things,
but relationships as well.
He may not require us to literally
give these things up,
but by agreeing to lay them all
at the foot of the cross,
we are saying that we are
willing and prepared
to give it all up for Jesus,
should He ask us to.

I was willing. I was even prepared.
I just had no way to truly understand
what that would feel like when it came
right down to it.
But God knows what is in our hearts.
He knew my heart that night,
and that I was indeed willing
to give it all up for Him.
And when the time actually came
for me to do this,
He gave me the grace to go through with it,
and what's more,
to look back with no regrets.

Early the next morning, John and I met with our assistant pastor and his wife. We shared what the Lord had spoken during the night. They didn't totally understand it all, but knew God was indeed calling us to step out for Him. Within just a few days, they had organized a Mission Support Team and began making inquiries as to how we would need to go about fulfilling this call on our lives.

John and I knew for certain only a few things.

1. We would be traveling a great deal.
2. We needed a motor home to do this traveling.
3. We would need to raise support.
4. We would be Holy Spirit led.

That's about all we knew for sure, but we were moving ahead at what seemed like break-neck speed. In early August, our church had a beautiful commissioning service for us. We also began to send out support letters for the ministry.

In September, a pastor called from the Columbia, South Carolina, area. He had heard about me through a friend and wanted a few copies of my book mailed to him. Shortly thereafter, he contacted me about coming to speak at a meeting for pastors and intercessors.

I spoke at that meeting, and all the pastors were asked to line up in the front as I gave them the words from the Lord. At least one of those words had a great impact on some of the pastors who were there. The Lord had given me a word in June of this year and I knew I was to share it at this meeting. The following is what God spoke to me —

> **I want all the pastors in the city**
> **to clear their schedules once a week,**
> **to meet together and pray for their nation,**
> **their city, and their state, in that order.**
> **They must come into this with**
> **clean hands and a clean heart.**

Four pastors of different denominations from the Columbia area began to meet the following week. A few other pastors have been added and they are still meeting every week.

A couple of months before this, God had instructed me to take that same word to four pastors in the Hickory, North Carolina, area. They were of four different denominations: Southern Baptist, Reformed Church of Christ, Assemblies of God, and Roman Catholic.

Those pastors received the word and one of them began to organize meetings, even to the extent of having a countywide prayer meeting, inviting all the pastors in the county. I thank God for shepherds who are willing to make the sacrifices necessary in order to be obedient to what He has asked them to do.

While all this was going on, the need for a motor home became an increasing reality, so John and I began the search. John and I had made a list of things we would need in a motor home. It was fairly detailed and we laid our hands on that list and prayed. We didn't need anything brand new or fancy, but if we were going to spend a significant amount of time on the road, certain things would be necessary. I recall clearly, the first night after we wrote out the list, I went back downstairs later that night and added one more thing to the bottom. I wanted the interior to be green.

We had gone through a lot of our resources by this time, due to John not having a job, and knew God was going to have to perform a miracle if we were to have the vehicle we needed. However, we weren't concerned about any of this. We just kept working on getting our house cleaned out and in order, knowing we were getting close to the time where we would be stepping out into the unknown, to follow what Jesus was calling us into. We also continued to do our homework, learning all we could about motor homes, so we would have a considerable amount of knowledge when the time came.

About two months later, in October, John saw a free want-ad paper on a table in the post office. He walked past it and then went back, feeling he should pick it up. Most of it was missing, but of course, the RV section was there. John had no idea, when he went back to get that paper, that it would be the key to our home for the next few years.

He read and re-read those want ads, finally circling four of them, then gave it to me. By this time, we had looked at quite a few for sale, checking out everything from small RV lots to large dealers, and some for sale by owner. The cost varied a lot, but all were quite expensive. The motor homes John had circled in this sale paper were fairly inexpensive, and I decided right away to not even call about one that was advertised at $10,000. Even though I wasn't looking for anything fancy, I felt certain this was not something that would be suitable.

Over the next few days, we went to look at the other three and found so many things wrong with them that we didn't even test-drive one. I finally decided to call about the one listed for $10,000. It was located 98 miles away from us, but we went to look at it anyway. The first thing I noticed was that the interior was green.

We went on a ride in it with the owner. It started quickly and had a smooth sound, even going up and down some big hills. The owner went through the entire unit with us. Everything worked! That was quite a shock. I don't believe we had seen even one where everything worked. Then we looked over receipts where repairs had been made and servicing had been done. There were only 60,000 miles on it and a car dolly came with it.

John and I told him we were definitely interested and we needed to go home and pray about it and see how much money had been raised. The next day we contacted him to see if he would sell it for any less. We agreed on $9,000. We didn't have that much money raised yet but a man at church made a donation of $1200 and loaned us the other $3300 to be paid back whenever it came in. It seemed God was in this as we watched everything come together so smoothly. The following day, John and I drove the 98 miles to purchase the motor home. After finishing the paperwork and hooking the car to the dolly, we began the long drive home. Freezing rain began to fall as we headed down the big mountain outside Asheville. I could tell John was very tense, but he handled it like a pro. We were so thankful to finally get back to the house safely.

Over the next week, we worked steadily, cleaning, shampooing the carpet, replacing the bathroom floor and getting everything in order to go. We still had no real idea of when we would be leaving, but felt so strongly that it would be soon.

The days were so busy I didn't have
a lot of time to process all this.
But during the night when I got up to pray,
I would look out the windows
into the backyard,
just looking at all the trees.
I loved those big, old trees.
I told the Lord I was going to
miss my trees.
And He said,
"Don't you think I have more
trees for you?"

Of course He did.
After all, when you get right down to it,
God owns all the trees,
just as He owns the cattle
on a thousand hills (Psalm 50:10).

But at the moment,
those trees didn't feel like they were mine...

One Year from Today

November 6th, 2011 was a warm Sunday afternoon. I felt drawn to be alone with the Lord, so I went out into the motor home, which was parked in the driveway. I must have sat there quietly for at least an hour, just waiting on the Lord. Finally, He spoke.

You have one year to call them to repent.

I waited. Nothing else. I asked, "One year from now, Lord?"

One year from today.

One year from today. The only thing that stood out to me about November 6th is that it is my son's birthday. Some time later, I shared this word with a pastor's wife. She called me back to ask if I realized what November 6th, 2012 was. No, I didn't.

"Election Day," she told me.

> *"One year from today."*
> *Deep in my heart I knew there was a*
> *great significance to this word.*
> *Greater than I wanted*
> *to think about.*
> *And the urgency of the call pressed on.*

January 2012

In January of 2012, I was driving home from my daughter's house in Knoxville, where I had been recovering from emergency surgery. The presence of God was evident in the car. I finally turned off the music, sensing the Lord was going to tell me something. I didn't have to wait long. The words were strong and clear.

> **I want them to step up to My throne.**
> **To come boldly to the throne of grace**
> **and cry out for mercy for their nation.**

I was trembling as I drove. The first thought I had was how the intensity had grown. From "life as we know it is about to change" to "cry out for mercy." I also knew when God said "them," He meant that word to be for pastors, leaders, and intercessors. Actually, for anyone who was willing to repent and intercede for this nation.

I had a strong sense that I was to give this word to a pastor on my trip home. I simply told the Lord that if I was supposed to stop at a church, to make it so plain to me that it would be right there (as I stretched my hand out toward the right side of the highway). Maybe a mile down the road, I saw it! The church was literally "right there." Just off the interstate and back down a little road.

I got off the exit and turned toward the church, calling John as I did so to let him know where I would be stopping.

I was just feeling strong enough to make the trip home. Driving into the parking lot, I realized how weak I still was, and prayed for the strength to get out of the car and walk inside.

Parking in the closest space to the church office, I got out and started walking toward the door. A man came out, heading for his truck. I asked him if the pastor was in. He told me the senior pastor was not, but he was one of the pastors and asked if he could help me.

Thank You, Lord! I didn't have to go up all those steps to the office. The timing was perfect. Another minute and that pastor would have been gone.

I told him how I came to be there and gave him the word from the Lord. He absolutely lit up! He was so excited as he shared about the urgency he had been feeling concerning the state of our nation and where we were headed. That word was confirmation to him and such an encouragement. He went on to say that he now felt released to share his growing burden for repentance with his church. After thanking me numerous times, we went our separate ways.

I continued driving home, not nearly so weak and tired as I had been before my stop.

I arrived home to an almost empty house. By this time, we had moved almost everything we were keeping into a storage unit and given away everything else. We were sleeping on our mattress and box springs, having given away our entire bedroom suite. A few boxes on the floor held what we needed and the closets were almost empty.

John and I
were not the least bit bothered
or concerned about these things.
We were that certain of the Lord's leading.
Our children, who are all adults,

were very concerned
when we began giving everything
away.
They felt we should at least sell it.
But God kept putting people
right in front of us
who needed specific things we had.
Knowing we wouldn't be
needing them much longer,
we just gave them away.
We had been divesting ourselves of
almost everything we owned for
about three months at this point,
only keeping personal things that
had real meaning for us.
The rest of it, after all, is just stuff.

Our house had been up for sale for almost a year. It was an older home in a nice neighborhood with four bedrooms and 32 trees on the property. The trees had been a big drawing point when we purchased this property. I have always loved trees, and was more concerned with giving up my trees than I was about the house.

About a week after I had arrived home, I was out running errands. John had stayed home. The worship music was turned up in the car and I was having a great time singing and praising the Lord. Then I heard His voice over the music.

I want you to give your house back to the bank.

"What??"

I want you to give your house back to the bank.

I turned off the music, thinking I must have misunderstood what God was saying to me. And the Lord spoke for the third time.

I want you to give your house back to the bank.

I began to tell God why we couldn't do that. You see, we had purchased our home ten years earlier and had put down almost 40%. I told Him that we would need the money if we were going into full time ministry. I asked Him why He couldn't just send a buyer. Even though John had been out of work, we weren't in foreclosure, or in a position where we had to give our home back to the bank.

John and I had actually managed quite well considering we had gone to one income when I resigned from my job, and then to unemployment after his job was eliminated. We didn't have a lot of debt, and had just cut back to trim down our spending. We saw God's hand in this, knowing we couldn't have managed nearly as well on our own.

No longer able to concentrate on what I was doing, I cut my errands short and headed home. I needed to tell my husband what God had told me. I felt certain that John would be in agreement with me about this.

As I pulled into the driveway, John came walking out, opening the car door for me when I stopped.

Immediately he said, "I have to tell you what God said to me."

I said, "I do, too, but you go first."

"God told me we are to give our house back to the bank."

I replied, "He told me the same thing! But you don't think we're really supposed to do it, do you?"

As I look back on this, I realize how totally
ridiculous it sounds!
Why I thought John and I could agree
to disagree with God,
I have no idea.
I was just thrown sideways by this,
and yet I knew it was God.
That's why I was so disturbed by it.
I knew God had spoken this to me.

Not once, but three times.
He obviously meant what He said...

John knew he had heard God and that settled it. Not for me! I got up every night for the next ten nights and told God over and over why this just wasn't a good idea. I had a whole list. I told Him how it wouldn't look good for us to go into ministry and not fulfill our obligations. What would people think? And last and possibly least, how we could really use the money when we started into full time ministry. I was still more concerned with what people would think than I was with the money. If God was calling us into ministry, He would take care of us. I was certain of that. I also asked Him over and over again, "God, why can't You just send a buyer. It would be so easy for You to just send someone to buy the house!"

Every night, God told me the same thing in the same kind voice.

These things don't matter, My child.
These things just don't matter.

Finally, I realized I was getting nowhere. I stopped getting up in the night to argue with God and I gave in. I'm not saying I was in agreement. I just gave in. I can't even tell you I was trying to be obedient or anything spiritual like that. I knew it wasn't an option anymore. I was resigned to the fact that John and I would do what God had told us to do whether we understood it or not. I knew we would just do it. John was much more settled about this than I was though. But then, I argue with God often, so I'm sure He wasn't surprised when I argued about something as big as giving our house back to the bank.

There is something very precious to me about this time in God's continual love and patience, no matter how many times I came to Him with my arguments. I'm not sure I could have been that patient had I been on the other side of this debate with one of my own kids. I hadn't told our children about what God had said. After all, supposing He changed His mind...

Finally, I knew I needed to call them. I called the girls first. They listened quietly and handled it very well. Then I called my son. I told him what God had said and how I had been getting up every night arguing with God about it.

"Why?" he wanted to know.

It's true, why would I pick this battle when we hadn't even questioned so many other seemingly strange things the Lord had asked of us. So I shared how I felt about going into full time ministry and not fulfilling our obligations. I told him my concerns about how this wasn't going to look good. I was amazed at my son's reply.

"Those things don't matter, Mom. Those things just don't matter."

I began to cry as I told him that was what God had said to me night after night. Almost word for word. My son continued to tell me how he saw us as forerunners. How things are changing rapidly and we are all going to have to learn to give things up, to let go of things. Oh, maybe not houses, but things. Things we thought we couldn't live without. And by the time many people are at the place where they have to make these sacrifices, our testimony will help to encourage them.

Well, by the time that phone call came to an end, I had a different mindset. I can't say I was thrilled about giving up our home, but I was okay with it. I was settled. Later that day, we called the bank and started the details of a deed in lieu, something we previously barely even knew existed.

Just a couple of days later, God told me we were to be on the road full-time by February 15th. Fortunately, we had been diligent to prepare ourselves for this moment, and there were only a few loose ends to tie up. Even though we didn't have a total picture of what God had called us to, we had continued to prepare. The last few days still were extremely hectic even though we had done so much ahead of time. The motor home was in the driveway ready to go and we began to move our last few personal things into it. The house was empty and clean and we spent the night in the motor home. We pulled out of our driveway for the last time on February 14th, 2012.

The Journey Begins

The clock read 3:40am. It was February 14ᵗʰ, 2012. I got out of bed to pray.

After spending some time praying, reading, and singing praises, a conversation from a couple of days earlier came to my mind. I felt the Lord was reminding me of what this friend had said to me. As I was leaving, he had simply said, "I love you." He knew we were heading out into the unknown and wanted to convey how he felt as a brother in Christ. It meant a lot to me at the time, and now it seemed God wanted to show me something in more depth about this. I thanked the Lord for Andrew's friendship and his kind words. Then God began to speak to me.

> **My child, you are going to be loved**
> **all over this nation.**
> **And hated as well.**
> **Be aware, My child,**
> **and have the proper response**
> **to both.**
> **Be prepared. You will see hate, even venom.**
> **And love in its truest form.**
> **Be prepared.**
> **And know they aren't hating you.**
> **It's Me they will hate.**
>
> **Just be prepared.**

Be prepared.

The Lord was warning me, preparing me for what would lie ahead. And yet while thanking Him, I didn't really have a clue what I would encounter.

John and I had no idea how we would feel knowing our only home was this "home on wheels." As we rolled out onto the highway, we were not prepared for the total peace that enveloped us. It was amazing! There was a grand excitement, too. We didn't know what lay ahead, but we knew God was leading us and that we were in His perfect will. That was the only thing that mattered.

I picked up a small stack of unopened mail and opened the envelope on top. It was a newsletter from David Wilkerson. He was talking about God calling Abraham. I read part of it out loud to John and we realized God had given us more confirmation and encouragement.

In Genesis we read,

¹Now the Lord said to Abram,
"Go forth from your country,
and from your relatives
and from your father's house,
to the land which I will show
you;
²And I will make you a great
nation, and I will bless you, and
make your name great;
and so you shall be a blessing;
³And I will bless those who bless you,
and the one who curses you I will
curse.
And in you all the families of
the earth will be blessed."
⁴So Abram went forth
as the Lord had spoken to him;
Genesis 12 :1-4a (NASB)

God called Abraham to go to a place
he knew not of. It felt like God was
calling us to a similar place, except
ours was a transient place.
A place of almost total unknown.
And even though God hadn't made any
promises to John and I except that He
would take care of us, that in itself was
enough.
The confidence that comes
from being obedient to His call
would carry us through.

Our first night on the road we parked in a Walmart parking lot. The next day, we found a campground. I was to speak in South Carolina to a group of intercessors in four days.

Those four days went by quickly and I soon found myself at the first meeting of our new journey.

The room was packed and I recognized only a few of the faces. Some had already read my book, but everyone appeared ready to hear the message.

I felt the anointing of the Lord immediately and, although I had notes, God brought to my mind exactly what I needed to tell them. It was a great meeting. I felt led to open it up for questions at the end and there was quite a bit of good discussion.

There was a lady who said she had read my book, but otherwise did not know me. In the wee hours of the morning on February 14th, God had awakened her and told her to pray for Maxie Hellmann. This was not a common occurrence for her, and she knew nothing about me other than that I was the author of a book she had read. Obediently, she prayed.

Tears filled my eyes as I realized that
while I was sleeping, God had awakened
someone who didn't even know me to
intercede on my behalf.
We must never underestimate

47

the power of intercession.
That is part of God's provision
in His promise
to protect and take care of us.
This was only the first of many times we
would cross thresholds into difficult
territory only to find that others had been
stirred
to do battle on our behalf.

There were others at that meeting who would become dear friends to me in the coming months and years. I am so thankful for each and every one of them.

The meetings continued to multiply in the Midlands of South Carolina. After we would speak to a group, there would be at least one person who would ask if we could speak to a group they were affiliated with. There were ladies' groups, pastors and intercessors, deacons with their wives, etc. Each group was different, but they were all such a blessing to us.

One woman I met at that first meeting, and who is still a close friend of mine today, asked if I would speak to a group of ladies. I rode with her to the meeting and at one point, while we were sitting at a stoplight, she turned to me and said, "You know Maxie, I'm sure you're tired. You have had meetings for days. I could have just told these ladies about you and given them the message God has given you, but they wouldn't have listened to me because I have a house. They will listen to you because you don't have a house."

And the light turned green...so she turned
her attention away from me and back to driving.
I was glad.
I needed a moment to digest that.
No one had been quite as blunt
as my new friend.
People would listen to me
because I don't have a house.
It still stung a bit.
It wasn't that I regretted

giving up our house,
but it was going to take a little getting
used to.
I knew there were a number of reasons
why God required this of us
and this was obviously one of those reasons.
More and more of His purpose would be
uncovered as time went on.

This meeting was very precious to me. The ladies were wonderful, quite receptive to the message of repentance for our nation. Near the end, one lady came around the table and handed me something wrapped in a tissue. She told me it was her favorite necklace, but God had told her to give it to me as a reminder that He would always have trees for me. I unwrapped the tissue to find a silver pendant with a beautiful tree carved out of it! The tears began to fall down my face as I looked into her eyes. She will never know what that meant to me. I wear it often, and always think of how great our Father is, and how He is mindful of us from the smallest detail to the largest giant in our lives. I almost feel as though God Himself placed that pendant into my hands.

At one of those first meetings, I recall a church deacon who said he had one question for us.

"What do you do on those days when you think, 'What have we done?'"

John and I looked at each other and then back at the gentleman.

We both answered, "We don't have those days. We don't even have those moments."

And it's true.
I don't believe there has
ever been even one moment
where my husband and I
thought we made a mistake.
Even in the difficult times,
there has still been such peace.

A peace that we
can't understand, but is
unmistakably present.
That, and seeing
God's hand in so many situations,
serves as
confirmation to us
that we did
indeed hear God calling us to this
strange and unusual
placeless place.

A few days before we left Columbia, I was just quietly sitting in the Lord's presence when I had a vision. I saw lightning, far away. Over and behind a huge mountain. I didn't see any trees on the mountain, just light grey rock. Then the Lord began to speak to me –

The storm is coming, My child.
It is still far away, but it's coming.
I am that Mountain and I am standing
between you and the storm,
but that Mountain will be removed if
things don't change and then the storm
will come.
It is still far off...but it is coming.

Many things are coming like as have
never been seen before.
You will experience much
but I will cover you.

Provision

The morning we were leaving the Columbia area, the Lord took us through a very interesting 24 hours. A pastor had asked us to meet him at a restaurant for breakfast on our way out of town.

While we were eating, the server stopped by our table to tell us our ticket had already been taken care of. The pastor began to look around to see who might have paid our bill. He didn't see anyone he knew and couldn't figure it out, but pushed a $20 bill across the table to us and said, "Well, I was going to buy your breakfast but I'll just give this to you for some gas instead." We thanked him and were soon on our way. At a meeting later that evening, two men we didn't know each gave us a $20 bill, as well.

The next morning, we stopped to get gas. Pulling up behind a small SUV, John and I got out of the motor home to speak to the man at the pump when he waved at us. He wanted to know if we were on vacation and, after telling him what we were doing, he waved for his wife to get out and come back to talk to us. We shared a bit and they were really excited. We got back inside to pull up to the pump and they pulled away. Before John could even get out to pump the gas, we heard a knock at the door. It was the gentleman, holding out a $20 bill.

"We wanted to buy you a gallon of gas," he said.

Hmmm...that made four $20 bills. We were clearly seeing God's hand in this.

Later in the day we were at an Arby's. John went to throw away our trash and bent down to pick something up in front of the trashcan. He came back to the table and held out a folded up $20 bill! We looked around. There was no one in the restaurant except us and the employees behind the counter! We didn't know how long that money had been there, but it was obviously intended for us.

Five $20 bills in 24 hours! God was indeed letting us know He would take care of us, and that it was most certainly going to be in some interesting ways.

"For I know the plans that I have for you,"
declares the Lord,
"plans to prosper you and not to harm you,
plans to give you a hope and a future.
Then you will call upon me
and come and pray to me,
and I will listen to you.
You will seek me and find me
when you seek me with all your heart."

Jeremiah 29:11-13 (NIV)

A Child Is Born

John and I arrived in Knoxville, Tennessee, just a short time before our daughter went in to have an emergency C-section. Although the baby was early, everything went fine and we were blessed with a new grandson, Judah Rhodes. A strong, Godly name for the strong Godly man he will grow up to be.

Almost as soon as we arrived in Tennessee, God began to put the book of Esther on my heart. I read through it quickly. As many times as I have read that book, and know it well, the excitement never dims. What an amazing story Esther is! The book, as well as the lady.

During this time, I woke up early one morning to the Lord asking me to get up. He had something to tell me. I don't share many of my personal times with the Lord in my books, because they are just that – personal. However, this is one I knew He wanted others to read. I believe God will use this section of the book to impact many lives. Below is our conversation.

> **This is your only opportunity, My child.**
> **If you want out, tell Me now.**
> **And yes, you will still go through the storm**
> **but I will protect you.**

> *I was speechless!*
> *Oh! The things that ran through my mind!*

Things like, this is a fine time to
ask me if I want out.
After we've given up everything!
We didn't even have a home
to go back to!
I felt like I was dangling
in the dark.
I simply could not comprehend
why He would ask me this question now.
But one thing I absolutely did know.
My Father understood the turmoil
I was experiencing at this moment.

"God, I don't understand. I mean, this isn't like a job that you just choose or turn down. Lord, have You called me? Will I make a difference?"

Of course I've called you!
You are My prophet.
Where you go, My child,
people will be saved.

I do not have anyone to take your place.
Of course, I have others.
But no one to take the place for what you
are going to do.

The time is too short.
I have groomed you for this for many years.
And I indeed called you before you were born.

But yes, you can step out if you wish,
if you choose.
If you want to lead a more normal life
I will set you up for that.
Just tell me.

"Lord, I know I'm called of You and I'm not sure I understand an opportunity to step out of that calling."

You will be hunted, My child.

Possibly put in prison.
But I will take care of you and yours.
All your children and your grandchildren.

And many others will be saved and covered as well.
You will not lose your life in this, but it won't be easy
and it won't always be what you are experiencing
now.

I just want to make sure you understand that.
It's going to get very hard before it's over.

But I will protect you.

Know and understand that I will protect you.
You can always hide in Me.

And it will always be rewarding —
even in the hard times.

"Lord, I feel like I made my choice a long time ago. I want to be in Your perfect will."

Then that is your answer, My child.
This is what you were created for.

Peace began to envelop me. It was settled. And I almost didn't hear that last line He spoke to me...

Our daughter, Candi, came home with Baby Judah just a few hours later. What can be better than a new grandbaby? Such joy, just to hold him, smell his sweet baby smells, rock him, and sing songs about Jesus to him. Thank You, Lord, for this blessing, and that we could be here to be a part of it.

It would be over a week before God came back to that last line.

This is what you were created for.

I was reading in *The Harbinger*, by Jonathan Cahn, before going to sleep. I was on page 244, almost finished with the book, when I read, *"It was all for this purpose, all for this time."* And all of a sudden I was broken. Feeling compelled to get out of bed and pray, I just knelt down and cried out to God.

This is what you were born for.

It had finally sunk in. And I was overwhelmed. I cried and cried, asking God to forgive me for not seeing it before. But there was really nothing to forgive. It was all revealed to me in His perfect timing.

> *To think that I was 54 years old*
> *and just now doing what*
> *I was born to do...*
> *What had I been doing for 54 years?*
> *Training.*
> *And as I look back I recognize how*
> *God had indeed been grooming me*
> *for such a time as this.*

And so I finished reading *The Harbinger*. What a book! There were so many things that spoke to me even on the last two pages.

> *A wall, a watchman, and a trumpet.*
> *A message...not exactly the kind that wins*
> *popularity contests.*
> *They will do everything they can*
> *to attack and discredit it.*
> *Otherwise, they would have to accept it.[1]*
> *The watchman must sound the alarm.*
> *No matter the cost.*

Charleston, South Carolina

And so we were back on the road. Blowing the trumpet, sounding the alarm, for all who would hear.

---

[1] (taken in part from *The Harbinger*, by Jonathan Cahn, pgs. 251-253)

A few days later, God had directed us to Charleston, South Carolina. We had been at the campground there for three nights with no limit of ministry opportunities. Neither John nor I felt God was quite finished with us there. After checking with the campground, we found it was already completely booked. Due to an event in town, so was everything else nearby. It would be necessary for us to pull out in the morning.

A little later in the day, we received a call inviting us to a meeting for pastors and intercessors, which would be held the following morning. Feeling God would have us to attend that, we made a decision to pack up and drive the motor home to the meeting, intending to leave the area immediately afterward.

I woke up at 1:08am to the Lord saying —

**My child, you aren't leaving Charleston today.
You'll see, but you aren't leaving yet.**

Well, I had certainly felt that, but had no idea how God would work it out since there didn't appear to be anywhere to park the RV. I would leave that up to Him and go back to sleep.

A few hours later, we were driving to that meeting, towing the car behind us. We didn't know anyone at the meeting, having been invited by a friend of a friend, but they welcomed us warmly. It lasted about two hours and was fairly uneventful until near the end when the Lord spoke to me.

People in the group had been talking about knocking down denominational walls (which sounded good to me). They kept discussing Charleston...Charleston...Charleston...and the coming revival. It seemed they felt it was all going to begin in Charleston and that Charleston would become the hub for a huge revival. I felt the familiar "fingernails on chalkboard" that comes to me when something just doesn't set well with my spirit. It all sounded good, but something was not quite right. Then the Lord spoke to me —

**They may be knocking down
walls of denominations,**

**but they need to be careful
not to put Charleston up on the
pedestal the denominations
are coming down from.**

You need to give them this word.

Oh no! We were just visitors here. I sure didn't want to have to give a word like that. But God didn't let up, so I told Him if a door opened I would do it. Of course, the opportunity came almost immediately and I gave the word. The leader was very gracious, telling me they received the word because of the humble spirit it was given in.

Thank You, Lord. I know I am only able to do this because of You.

At the close of the meeting, we were getting up to leave when a few of those in attendance came over to speak with us. A young man came up and asked where we would be Sunday morning. We had to tell him we were leaving town because there was no availability at any of the campgrounds. He then said he knew we were supposed to speak at his church on Sunday and that the church had all the hook ups for the RV we would need. Wow! It is simply amazing how God accomplishes His will. We were able to establish a good connection with this pastor, having time to visit with him and meet for prayer.

Such an anointing poured down on Sunday morning. As I shared the message God had given me about repentance, people were wiping their eyes all over the sanctuary. At the close of the service, the pastor came up to talk about repenting. He could hardly speak and finally just broke down. He asked everyone to kneel at their seats and repent. As I looked across the room, every person was kneeling! Yes, I believe something was accomplished here this morning. Thank You, Lord, for allowing us to be a part it.

Are You Prepared?

In April I began to feel a shift. The Lord was still speaking to me about the nation repenting and turning back to Him, but now it seemed there was more.

In April of 2012, the Lord gave this word to me.

> **There is a huge storm coming to this nation.**
> **Not necessarily a physical storm,**
> **but a storm nonetheless.**

On May 3rd, I had been awake most of the night. I had such a burden for many things. I had been praying and reading my Bible and then all of a sudden at 4:40am the Lord began to speak to me.

> **I have a message for you.**
> **Hard times are coming.**
> **Prepare, prepare, prepare.**
>
> **If they are not prepared,**
> **many won't make it.**
>
> **Many will lose everything,**
> **but they can save their lives**
> **and their families**
> **if they will only listen.**

Prepare, My child.
They must prepare.
Even the animals prepare
for the seasons.

It's a requirement, My child,
not a suggestion.

They must prepare in the Word
and in their relationship with Me.

Study, memorize, spend time with Me.

Learn to hear My voice clearer
than the person closest to you.

Prepare.

Those who aren't prepared
won't make it.

Get your mind off things that
have no eternal value.

Stop spending money unnecessarily.
Simply stop.

Stop running to and fro as though
you don't know what you're doing.

Prioritize your time and
spend most of it with Me.

You may think you're prepared.
Think again.

Wow! What a word! I don't believe that needs any commentary from Maxie. It speaks for itself.

During the next few weeks as I shared this word with people, there were many varied responses, but more often than not I heard comments about how those who were storing up food and other things were going to protect what they had. People were asking me questions about guns and how to keep things safe from those who hadn't prepared.

On June 25th, the Lord spoke to me about this.

> **Those who have prepared out of a wrong heart will not be using what they have stored up.**

> **The righteous will get it. I will see that the righteous get it.**

We need to understand that much of our preparation is for the harvest the Lord is going to bring in. He wants to use us to help bring in the harvest. You can't talk to your neighbor about Jesus if you don't feed her hungry three-year-old first.

There have been people in every group I have spoken to who have come up to me afterward to thank me for coming to tell them about these things. God has been speaking to others, all across this land, about the judgment that is coming and showing them how they need to prepare.

God has told some to collect blankets and warm clothing, some to get Bibles, medicine, and other necessities. Just about all of them have felt led to store up food and water. I have talked with people who have their garage and basement completely full, with a detailed strategy of rotating things so nothing gets out of date. And others have felt they were only supposed to have a little extra food and water.

Unfortunately, there are many who don't want to hear any of this. Just about everyone who has talked to me about preparing has at least one story of their family, friends, pastor, or church belittling them for what they are doing. They have been so thankful to have some confirmation and encouragement for what they truly felt God was telling them to do.

My child, listen to me and treasure my
instructions, tune your ears to wisdom, and
concentrate on understanding. Cry out for insight
and understanding. Search for them as you would
for lost money or hidden treasure. Then you will
understand what it means to fear the Lord,
and you will gain knowledge of God.
For the Lord grants wisdom!
From his mouth come knowledge
and understanding.

Proverbs 2:1-6 (NLT)

Michigan and the Messenger

On Saturday, July 14th, the Lord began to put Michigan on my mind. I took my dog, Moses, for a long walk, and talked to the Lord. I told him we didn't know anyone or have any contacts in Michigan. Of course, He already knew that, and I knew this journey had been Holy Spirit led from the beginning, but somehow Michigan seemed strange to me.

I still had two meetings scheduled before we could head north, but on July 17th, 2012, John and I had picked up our grandson, Elijah, and we were on our way to Michigan. Elijah was 12 years old at the time, and excited about going on a mission trip with us.

The first night, God led us to a small campground in West Virginia. It wasn't a place we normally would have stopped, but we felt a strong sense that was where we should spend the night.

The next morning, we had intended to get on the highway right after breakfast, but John and I both felt that we needed to go into the little town just a few miles from the campground. John unhooked the car and we drove into town. McDonald's kept coming to my mind. Yes, a biscuit and coffee sounded good, but I knew that wasn't why God was taking us there. We passed a small library that I felt drawn to, but I could see the yellow arches just down the street, so on we went.

While John and Elijah ordered, I stood off to the side, trying to be sensitive to the Holy Spirit in all the chaos of a busy McDonald's. But the chaos melted away as God directed my gaze to look at a lady sitting alone in a booth.

That's her.
She's the reason you're here.

I felt I needed to give her a Bible, so I went back to the car to get one. A book was on top of the Bibles. I didn't even remember putting it there. The title was something about Jesus loving us through the hard times. I put it aside to get to the Bibles, but felt very drawn to that book. I knew that's what God wanted her to have.

Carrying the book back inside, I walked over to the lady and introduced myself.

Then I told her, "God brought me to this McDonald's especially for you. He told me to give you this book and He wants you to know He loves you very much."

With that she burst into tears. She kept running her finger across the letters of the title on the book. Then she began to tell me how she had just lost her father and she was going through a really rough time.

She said, "You have no idea how badly I needed you to come in here this morning. Thank you so much for the book and for the message from the Lord."

After getting her permission, I prayed for her, gave her a hug, and we left.

Did all that take me out of my
comfort zone? You bet it did.
Yes, even me, after all the strange things
God has asked me to do.
But to see that lady caress the cover of that
book, and smile at me through her tears
was worth it ten times over.

Get out of your box!
Knock down those comfort zones
and go on an errand for God!
Not only will someone else be blessed,
but you will find the greatest blessing
is yours.

On our way back to the campground, we had to pass the library again. I asked John to stop there. As we got out of the car, my grandson asked what we were going to do. I told him we were giving them a copy of my book and taking some Bibles in. John didn't think they would be able to accept the Bibles, but we took them in anyway.

Speaking to the ladies behind the counter, we introduced ourselves and told them we were traveling across the country calling America back to God. I handed them a signed copy of my book. They seemed excited about it and said it would go on their shelf, as they argued over which one got to read it first.

Then we asked if we could donate some Bibles. We had a stack of nice Bibles, from children's all the way to large print. We asked if they could give the Bibles to anyone who came in and wanted one. They seemed very surprised that we wanted to give them the Bibles. After checking with the lady in the office, she gave us the thumbs up sign and thanked us for what we were doing.

Our grandson stood there watching all this and when we got back outside he said, "What just happened in there? I can't believe they took the Bibles!"

Well, after all, God did send us in there. I was so thankful Elijah recognized something unusual had taken place in that library and I knew, although he didn't totally understand, he had given God the credit for making it happen.

After arriving in Michigan, the Lord led us not only to the town He wanted us in, but also the campground. We know this in part because neither the area nor the campground were what we would have chosen.

Unsure of what exactly God wanted us to do, we spent time with our grandson, prayed, and waited on direction. It seemed like a long time, but was only a day and a half later when I knew God was leading me to drive into town. We needed a few things from the grocery store; however, I knew that wasn't why I was making that trip. I drove the ten miles into town by myself, needing the time alone with the Lord.

There was very poor cell phone reception at the campground, so upon arriving at the store, I decided to return a couple of phone calls before going inside. In the middle of a conversation with a pastor, I watched as two ladies (one older, and the other possibly her daughter) walked toward a pickup truck parked two spaces over from me. The pastor was speaking into my left ear...and the Holy Spirit was speaking into my right. I quickly told the pastor I would have to call him back, got out of the car and headed toward the pickup truck. I had no idea of the details, just that God wanted me to speak to those ladies.

The younger one had helped the older lady into the truck and was standing by the door when I walked up to them. I introduced myself, telling them I was a chaplain and that sometimes God gives me messages for people. About that time, I realized there was an older man with them as he was climbing into the driver's seat.

He had heard me and leaned over to say, "So what are you gonna tell us? That we won the lotto or something?"

"No sir. Nothing like that." I replied as I'm thinking, "God, what do you want me to tell them?"

About that time my mouth opened and what came out may have shocked me as much as it did them. I suppose what shocked me most was not the words but the authority they were spoken with. I barely recognized it as my voice.

"In the days to come the only thing that will help you is God!"

The younger lady, who was possibly in her 40s, was just staring at me and the man was quiet. I thanked them for their time and told them to have a blessed day before returning to my car.

I know there was more I could have
said or at least stuck around
in case they had questions
(which I'm sure they did),
but God did not tell me
to say anything more.
We have to be very careful
not to add our own commentary
to a word from the Lord.
I believe many messages from the Lord
are buried under the "words"
that we feel are necessary
to help explain what
God is saying.

I will never forget what God told me
a number of years ago,
after I had met with a pastor
to give him a word from the Lord,
and then shared a few of my own words.

God was very firm as He let me know
that was not what He had sent me in there for,
and the pastor would dwell on
what I had said,
not what God had wanted him to hear.
I quickly repented for my mistake that day
and knew I was forgiven.
If we just do our part,
God will take care of the rest.

Later, as I talked to the Lord about those people in the pickup truck, He clearly told me, the way that message was delivered, they will never forget it. And that the day will come when their backs will be against the wall and they will remember the word and cry out to Him.

After doing my shopping, I headed back to the campground. It wasn't a pretty drive and I wasn't really looking forward to it. The entire area seemed to be sad and oppressed. As I drove, I thought there were two words to describe it – sad and sadder.

As I came upon a church to my left, I recognized that familiar stirring in my spirit. I turned into a side street and stopped, asking the Lord if He wanted me to go back. Yes. I knew I had to go back to that church. I pulled into the parking lot and stopped near a well-dressed gentleman who was standing at the back of a car. Getting out, I asked if the pastor was around. He told me the pastor wasn't there. Still not sure why I was there, I asked if he would give the pastor a copy of my book. I signed one and handed it to him. He thanked me and started to say more when his phone beeped. He excused himself and stepped back to take the call.

As I turned back toward my car, I noticed an Asian man walking toward me. He was dressed very nicely with a long overcoat over his suit and wearing a top hat. He stopped about three feet from me, put his hands behind his back, and bowed ever so slightly toward me. He was wearing small, round, wire rimmed glasses and looked me straight in the eye as he asked, "So, what is the Lord saying?"

I thought it was really strange someone would walk up and begin a conversation like that. Thinking back for a moment, I wondered if I might have said something to the other man that would have led him to ask me that question, but nothing came to my mind. Besides, he hadn't been anywhere near us. I wasn't even sure where he came from. I hadn't seen him until he walked right up to me.

The word God had given me to take to the pastors in Hickory, North Carolina, is what came to me. God had recently spoken that word to me again.

> **Life as we know it is about to change.**
> **If there is anything you need to repent of,**
> **anything at all between you and God,**
> **you need to take care of it.**

"That's a good word. A very good word," he said, and then asked if I knew what was coming. I simply told him God had not given me details.

It was at that point when he said, "Let me tell you what the Lord is saying to me."

**There is a huge storm coming to this nation.
Not necessarily a physical storm,
but a storm nonetheless.**

"Yes! Yes!" I replied.

This was exactly what God had spoken to me just a few short weeks ago. It was written in my journal. In my excitement I had taken a step toward him and he stepped back, careful to keep that three feet or so between us.

Then he said, "And let me tell you the other thing God has been speaking to me. "We must prepare."

Once again I said, "Yes! God has been telling me that, too!"

He didn't seem at all surprised that I was hearing the same thing he was. As a matter of fact, he acted as though he had expected it. Like he already knew what I had heard from God.

"And I need to tell you one last thing," he said. "We don't have long to prepare."

"That's right." I told him. I stepped toward him again and he carefully stepped back.

I stood there for a moment trying to process all this. Finally, I spoke. "What are the chances that my husband and I would drive all the way from South Carolina to Michigan, and that I would be on this road and stop at this church..." as I trailed off, not knowing what else to say.

"No chance, Ma'am. No chance."

*I thanked him, told him good-bye, got in my
car and left. I was tingling from head to
toe as I drove out of the parking lot.
Was that man real? Was he a messenger? An angel?
I am still not sure of all that took place.
But I know I had an encounter that day.
I have had many divine appointments...this was that
...and more.*

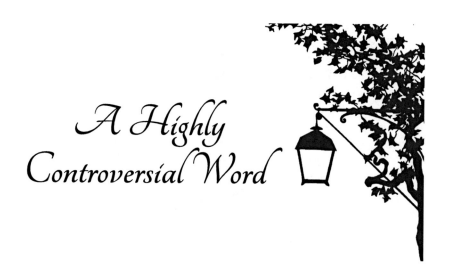

A Highly Controversial Word

On July 13th, 2012, the Lord gave me a word. It was very simple and to the point.

I want you to delete your Facebook account.

Nothing more. Just that. I had enjoyed Facebook, and had made a number of good ministry contacts from it. I knew God hadn't told me to delete the account because I was spending too much time on Facebook. Truthfully, I thought an awful lot of it was just plain silly. Who cares when you are going to brush your teeth, etc., etc. Mostly, I just stayed on for many of the same reasons others do – to see pictures of my grandchildren that are posted and to connect with friends from the past.

But God had spoken and that was that. Facebook would have to go. I knew I needed to put a couple of posts on to let people know I would be closing my account and why, so I did that. There were some replies to my post, and even phone calls. Some wanted to know if they should get off of Facebook too. I hadn't even thought about that! God had just spoken that word to me personally. All I could say was that each person needs to ask the Lord about what they should do. And that I would let them know if the Lord told me anything more about Facebook.

A few days later, after I thought most people had had a chance to read the posts about why I was closing my account, I began to try to delete it. I found it wasn't so easy.

I was busy during this time, on the road, meetings, etc. Seldom did I have a stable internet connection. Finally, on the night of July 28th, I knew I couldn't go to bed without getting that thing deleted! After trying multiple times, I was finally able to reach my daughter, who assured me she would get it deleted. I received a text a while later letting me know she had taken care of it. (I'm sure it's still out there somewhere, but I knew I had done all I could do.)

On August 2nd around 2am, I was awake and praying, when I felt so strongly that God was going to release another important word and that Hickory, North Carolina, was going to be the first to get it. I was scheduled to speak at a church in the Hickory area on August 12th. I wondered if that was where the word would first be released.

I had no idea how controversial
that word would be.
Or how many friendships
would be strained
and even shattered
because of it.

I never dreamed a church
would even cancel a meeting
over that word!

And I am still shocked
over the horrible things
said against me
because of that word.

But it isn't like God didn't
warn me...

It was 5:36am on August 6th when I woke up. I sensed the Lord's presence, and He began to speak to me.

Why don't you get up, My child,
and we'll talk for a while?

I picked up my Bible and journal and went out to the kitchen
table. For some reason this morning I was wide awake.
Sometimes when God wakes me up, I'm still so sleepy that I
stumble into things as I make my way into the other room, but I
believe I sensed something this morning. It seemed I was on high
alert as I sat down with my pen and journal to scribe what the
Lord was about to say to me.

I want all believers off Facebook.

My child, Facebook is an addiction.
And it's doing more harm than
drugs and alcohol combined,
because it's accepted, it's legal,
and it's free.

Marriages are falling apart
and children are being neglected
and even abused.

Countless, countless hours
are being stolen from Me.

There will come a time when
all those people would give
anything to have that time back,
but of course it is gone –
forever.

Tell this everywhere you go,
My child.

You will not be popular for it,
but I will cause conviction to rise up
in the hearts of people,
and many will turn back to Me
and break away.

They are tracking Christians
even now, on Facebook.

It will be a huge tool for the enemy
when the persecution moves in.

All I could think was...
This must be the word.

"Lord, I'm Amazed by You"

The first place this word was released was at a church in
Conover, North Carolina. The pastor had asked me to speak to
his Sunday School class first, and then the worship service. There
were around 100 people in the first group. They listened intently
as I shared the history of how John and I came to where we are
today.

About halfway through this class, I began having terrible pains all
across my stomach. It got worse and worse. I had never
experienced anything like it before.

The pastor asked if I would answer some questions at the end
and I know God gave me the answers because I was in such pain
by that point I could barely concentrate.

A lady came up to me at the end of that meeting and wanted to
ask me something.

I said, "Sure."

She asked me what the first and last name was of the person we
still owed $3000 to for the motor home.

I was more than a little surprised. I never shared that
information and she interpreted the look on my face correctly.

"No, you didn't mention anything about that," she said. And then
she went on. "You see, God woke me up the other night and told

74

me I should ask you for the first and last name of the person you still owe $3000 to for the motor home. And then he gave me the name of that person and I wrote it down in my journal. God also told me that if the name you gave me matched the name He had given me, I was to write you a check for the $3000 so you and John could pay off the loan."

I gave her the name.

"That's it!" she said. "I'll show you my journal."

And she ran off to write the check. I just stood there and stared at her back as she headed to her seat.

Yes. This really happened.
I have told my husband
and a couple of others who
are close to me,
that people are simply not
going to believe
many things in this book.
I'm sure this is near the top of the
"many things."

I have seen God do so much,
and I never cease
to be amazed.

The worship service was great! I gave all the words God had instructed me to give those wonderful people. I feel many of them were overwhelmed and got more than they bargained for possibly, but I know God will use it if they will allow Him to. We had a beautiful time around the altar at the end of the service.

The pains across my stomach continued, but they weren't quite as strong. Or maybe, I had just gotten used to them. Whichever it was, I was able to concentrate and truly felt the anointing, power, and authority of the Lord, as I spoke out what He had given me.

About thirty minutes after the service ended, the pains went away completely.

The following morning, I felt different somehow. I couldn't explain it, but it didn't feel small. It felt huge!

I wrote in my journal, *"I am in a strange and wonderful place today. I feel blessed at simply everything."*

John told me it was pouring over onto him.

The next night the Lord was talking to me. He told me many personal things, but one thing I especially found interesting.

Something has been birthed in you.
It will flow over into your ministry,
of course, but the real
birthing was in you.

So now I understood those
strange pains
all across my abdomen.
They were birthing pains.
I have heard others speak of this,
but it has never happened to me.
And though I do not
understand it fully,
I know something has taken place
within me that only God
could do.

Under His Wings

It was September 6th at 1:52am and I had been up praying for a while. The Lord began to speak to me.

> **There is a deceiving spirit closing
> in on your nation, My child,
> threatening to suffocate
> each and every one.**
>
> **My children *must, must* move
> closer to Me every day,
> must keep moving forward
> if they are to be free of this
> deceiving spirit.
> It is a very powerful spirit,
> My child.**
>
> **It will suck everyone in
> who is not pressing in to Me.**
>
> **Stay covered.
> Stay close.**

I was not surprised when God spoke this to me. What does surprise me, however, is how many people have already fallen into this trap of being deceived. I talk to people every day who call themselves Christians. I believe they love the Lord. But they have not been walking close enough to Him to keep their hearts and minds clear. Therefore, they are now seeing and hearing things through the fog. They are unable to determine what is truth and what is a lie. If something is only partly true, it is not truth. Often, what we hear today, even from the pulpit, is just enough truth to be dangerous. We must take everything we hear or read back to God. We must make sure it lines up with the Bible. If something is contrary to what the Bible says, it is not truth.

Our world is a mess and it is only getting worse by the day. I ask God frequently to keep me from being deceived. None of us is exempt from being deceived, from believing a lie. Truth is almost non-existent today except in the word of God.

I want to share one of my favorite passages of scripture.

[1]HE THAT DWELLETH IN THE SECRET PLACE OF THE MOST HIGH SHALL ABIDE UNDER THE SHADOW OF THE ALMIGHTY.
[2]I WILL SAY OF THE LORD, HE IS MY REFUGE AND MY FORTRESS:
MY GOD; IN HIM WILL I TRUST.
[3]SURELY HE SHALL DELIVER THEE FROM THE SNARE OF THE FOWLER,
AND FROM THE NOISOME PESTILENCE.
[4]HE SHALL COVER THEE WITH HIS FEATHERS,
AND UNDER HIS WINGS SHALT THOU TRUST:
HIS TRUTH SHALL BE THY SHIELD AND BUCKLER.
[5]THOU SHALT NOT BE AFRAID FOR THE TERROR BY NIGHT;
NOR FOR THE ARROW THAT FLIETH BY DAY;
[6]NOR FOR THE PESTILENCE THAT WALKETH IN DARKNESS;
NOR FOR THE DESTRUCTION THAT WASTETH AT NOONDAY.
[7]A THOUSAND SHALL FALL AT THY SIDE,
AND TEN THOUSAND AT THY RIGHT HAND;
BUT IT SHALL NOT COME NIGH THEE.
[8]ONLY WITH THINE EYES SHALT THOU BEHOLD
AND SEE THE REWARD OF THE WICKED.
[9]BECAUSE THOU HAST MADE THE LORD,
WHICH IS MY REFUGE, EVEN THE MOST HIGH,
THY HABITATION.

¹⁰THERE SHALL NO EVIL BEFALL THEE,
NEITHER SHALL ANY PLAGUE COME NIGH THY
DWELLING.
¹¹FOR HE SHALL GIVE HIS ANGELS CHARGE OVER
THEE, TO KEEP THEE IN ALL THY WAYS.
¹²THEY SHALL BEAR THEE UP IN THEIR HANDS,
LEST THOU DASH THY FOOT AGAINST A STONE.
¹³THOU SHALT TREAD UPON THE LION AND ADDER:
THE YOUNG LION AND THE DRAGON SHALT THOU
TRAMPLE UNDER FEET.
¹⁴BECAUSE HE HATH SET HIS LOVE UPON ME,
THEREFORE WILL I DELIVER HIM:
I WILL SET HIM ON HIGH, BECAUSE HE HATH
KNOWN MY NAME.
¹⁵HE SHALL CALL UPON ME, AND I WILL ANSWER HIM;
I WILL BE WITH HIM IN TROUBLE;
I WILL DELIVER HIM, AND HONOUR HIM.
¹⁶WITH LONG LIFE WILL I SATISFY HIM,
AND SHOW HIM MY SALVATION.

PSALM 91 (KJV)

Friends, I want to talk to you
for a moment.
I know, some of you are thinking
I've been talking to you for
a lot of pages now.
Well, yes, that's true,
but if you don't take anything
else to heart from this book,
please, get ahold of this.

There are sixteen verses
in Psalm 91.
The last fifteen are promises given to us
as children of God.
They are all miraculous,
supernatural,
promises,
of salvation, protection, provision.
He's got it covered.
Whatever His kids have need of,
He will provide it.

But let's get back to the first verse.
"He that dwelleth in the secret place
of the most High
shall abide under the shadow
of the Almighty."

Friends, in order to be on the
receiving end of those promises,
we have to
"dwell in that place."
And in order to
"dwell in that place,"
we must spend time with God.
We must talk to Him
and listen for His voice.
We must read His word
and we must be obedient
to what He is telling us.

If you have been a "Sunday Christian"
up until now,
if you have been lukewarm,
or riding the fence, only going to God
when you need something,
you desperately need to
change some things in your life.

If you are holding onto "little sins"
that you think aren't important,
things you don't want to let go of,
ask the Lord to help you.
If you are sincere in letting go
of those things,
He will help you to be victorious.
There is no time to waste!
I believe if we do not get
serious with God soon,
that deceiving spirit
will be so powerful,
it will be very difficult
to break through and understand

what is truth and what is not.

Or possibly,
you have never truly asked
Jesus to forgive you of your sins,
come into your heart,
and be the Lord of your life.
You can do that right now.
Just simply ask Him.

At the end of the day
the only thing that really matters,
is whether or not we have
a good relationship with God.

Would you all stop for a moment
to pray with me right now?

Oh God,
we need You so much.
We simply aren't able, in our own strength
to be the people You want us to be.
Help us, Lord, to desire a closer
relationship with You.
Help us to prioritize our time.
Draw us close to You
so we will not be deceived
into believing lies of the enemy.
Help us not to believe that
evil is good,
and good is evil.
One day we will all
have to stand before You, God.
Help us to be the people
You want us to be
before that day.
In Jesus' name.
Amen.

He who has
My commandments
and keeps them
is the one who loves Me;
and he who loves Me
will be loved by My Father,
and I will love him
and will disclose Myself to him.

John 14:21 (NASB)

Heading West

I woke up in the night to hear God say to me —

I want you to get on I-40 and head west.

The only thing I could think was, "How far, God?" He was faithful to answer —

Until it ends.

I thought He meant until I-40 ends; now I am wondering if it was to mean until the journey ends. I'm still not sure and I don't suppose it matters. I knew the time to leave was not immediate and that God would tell us when it was time. He was just giving us a "heads up," so to speak.

It was 14 months later that we would get on Interstate 40 and head west.

We were leaving from our daughter and son-in-law's house in Knoxville, Tennessee. After John got the Honda hooked up for towing, we were ready to go. Michael, Candi, and their three-year-old daughter and six-month-old son came out to pray for us. They just surrounded us and began to pray. Then Michael saw a picture of something the Lord was showing him. I call that picture "The Wake." This is how he described it.

"I see a big river and you guys are driving the motor home right through it. The wake behind the Honda is tremendous!"

"The wake is where must of the action will happen. Not necessarily while you are there but, after you leave, God will continue to do mighty things from the seeds you have planted."

"You may not know a lot of what has taken place until you get to heaven."

We still carry that picture in our hearts today. Although God has allowed us to see or hear much of what has happened as we travel from place to place, we treasure the thought of what is taking place in the wake.

Right before we left, our little granddaughter, Elianna, went over to where her Pop-Pop was bent down checking on the towing dolly, and laid her little hand on his shoulder to pray for him. Then she came to pray for me.

At this point in our journey
we had seven grandchildren.
What a blessing
to know their parents were teaching
them to pray for us
on a regular basis.
I believe
God holds the prayers
of little children
in a special place
in His heart.

This was a major step of faith in our journey. The cost to travel such a long way in a large vehicle can add up rapidly and we had no family, scheduled meetings, or pastors and churches to connect with along the way.

Although donations were coming in, we didn't have anywhere near enough money to go on a journey of this magnitude, but we left that in God's hands and headed west.

Nashville, Tennessee

A friend had asked us to stop outside Nashville to speak with a pastor there. We arranged to meet him at Panera and sat outside at a table talking with him for quite a while. He was a nice guy and seemed to be doing a great work for the Lord, but I didn't necessarily feel like this was a God appointment.

Shortly after he left, we realized why we were really there. An older couple that had taken a table next to us hesitantly came over to our table. They apologized, but told us they couldn't help but overhear our conversation and felt like God had brought them to that very restaurant to meet with us. We soon learned they had been hearing the same things from God that we were, but their friends and others at their church were just brushing them off. They were so thankful and encouraged by talking with us. When we parted they were going to go talk with their pastor. I pray they were well received.

> *No one wants to hear that judgment is coming.*
> *But we are much better off*
> *to listen, and be obedient,*
> *than to stick our head in the sand.*

Almost every time we stopped, whether it be for gas, at a rest stop, or some place else, God would speak to me. It would be something like —

> **I want you to go speak to that man at the next pump. I have a word for him.**

Or...

> **Do you see the lady sitting in that booth by herself? She needs you to go pray with her.**

Or maybe...

**You need to give that girl a Bible.
I want you to tell that boy that I love him and
I haven't forgotten about him.**

These were just a few of the words God spoke to me as we covered those miles westward.

There were many reactions as I spoke to people, but not once did I wonder if I had indeed heard God about speaking to each and every one. Some burst into tears, sharing something they had been struggling with, some sincerely thanked me, a few even grabbed me and hugged me with all their might.

I have no idea how many Bibles John and I gave out, how many people received a word from God, or the number of those we prayed for on that trip. It would have been difficult to keep count. I only know that every time John parked that motor home, there was someone God wanted to touch, and we were so blessed to be a part of it.

Arkansas

Driving mainly during the daylight hours, we spent the majority of our nights in Walmart parking lots. There was one particular day where we were feeling rather weary and decided to stop at a campground. I called quite a few that were on our route, but they were either full or couldn't accommodate a rig as long as ours. Finally, we stopped at a rest stop just for a break. Notices had been posted inside advising drivers to take a detour a little farther down the highway because of road construction. After getting back on the road, we made the decision to take the detour. We were just too tired to risk getting stuck in traffic.

Before we even came to the exit where we were to get off for the detour, the Lord began to impress something upon me and then I could "see" a church. It was to my right as we were traveling down the road. The lights were on and there were cars in the parking lot. God was telling me we were to stop there and ask if we could just park the motor home in their parking lot for the night.

I shared this with John about the time we got off the exit ramp. We drove quite a while along a narrow two-lane road with a swamp on either side. It was getting dusky and I knew John was so weary. I kept looking for that church the Lord had shown me. It had to be somewhere along this route. The vision was clear and there was no doubt in my mind what God had said about us stopping there.

Then I saw it! I was so excited! Finally, we could stop and settle in for the night. The church was on a corner and John pulled into the parking lot from the side street. A man came out from a building that looked like it might be a fellowship hall. He walked up to the passenger side of the motor home and I slid my window open to talk to him. Briefly telling him our dilemma of not being able to find a campground, I asked if we could park in their parking lot just for the night. He told me they had a program going on and needed their parking spaces.

I was totally caught off guard. I couldn't understand it. If God had shown me this church and told me to ask them if we could park there, why on earth wouldn't this man allow us to?

I wasn't sure what to say for a minute. Trying to buy a bit of time, I asked the guy if they had something going on for their youth. There was a lot of noise and activity coming from what appeared to be the fellowship hall.

"No," he said. "We are having a program called 'The Hereafter'. It's not just for the youth."

"Oh," I said. I could tell he was getting impatient for us to move on, so I thanked him anyway and John began to pull out of the parking lot. Just as we were turning onto the street, the Lord spoke to me.

They turned away My prophet.

Oh! I felt that deep inside and actually started to cry for that church and the leadership.

"God, please give them another chance," I cried as we went on down that dark road. "Give them one more chance."

A few miles farther, we came to a Walmart where we parked for the night. I was still distressed for that church. The man who turned us away wasn't the pastor, but ultimately I knew the pastor would be responsible for what took place there.

God didn't ever promise me He would give them another chance. However, He is full of grace and mercy. I still believe He would give them more than one opportunity, but then again, we don't know how many opportunities they have had already.

We need to be very careful to be sensitive to what God would have us to do. Whether it be buying someone a cup of coffee, a meal, or even a place to stay. We must be obedient to the Lord's voice.

From time to time, that church still comes back to me.
The man who turned us away had no idea if
we knew the Lord or not.
The Lord didn't lead me to mention
we were traveling ministers.
We could have been as lost as a goat in tall weeds,
desperately needing to come inside
to hear the program about the
hereafter.
Oh God, help us to be sensitive
to those You send to us
and those you send us to.

Simple Obedience

While driving through Arkansas, we passed a church on our right. God spoke to me about stopping there. John got off at the next exit and we found our way back to that church.

Knowing I needed to give the pastor a word from the Lord, I asked John to pray while I went inside. It was late Sunday afternoon, and I had no way of knowing if the pastor was even there, but a few cars were in the parking lot.

A young lady was on her cell phone in the foyer, so I walked over to the sanctuary doors and looked through the glass. It looked like a few people were having a small, informal meeting. I turned around and waited for the girl to get off the phone. When she saw I was waiting for her, she hung up, apologizing to me.

Handing her a prayer card, with our picture and a description of our ministry on it, I told her what my husband and I were doing.

Then I said, "Would it be possible for me to speak with your pastor for just a moment? I have a word from the Lord for him."

She said, "Sure. He's in there, but they are just having a meeting about the Christmas play. I'll go get him."

When the young lady came back out, I could tell by her face something was wrong. She was obviously embarrassed and her eyes began to fill up with tears as she told me the pastor had said I could wait or come back tomorrow.

She said, "I'm so sorry. We believe in that here and I know you're for real. I don't know why he wouldn't come out for a moment."

I gave her a hug and thanked her for trying. She asked if it would be all right if she prayed for me and, after the sweetest prayer, I bid her good-bye.

Oklahoma

John and I didn't make decisions (on where to stop or where to stay) because it looked good or if we thought we'd like a particular place better than another. We were led by the Holy Spirit at every town, every campground, and every Walmart. Even gas stations and restaurants were almost always because God had spoken to us or we felt led to go there.

God led us to a campground outside of Oklahoma City and told us we were to stay there for four days. We drove into the small town nearby and began to walk around the little downtown area and pray. God led us into a small gift shop where a lady who worked there asked where we were from. I shared with her that my husband and I were traveling across the United States calling people to repent and turn back to God. She got really excited and told me I had to meet her son. She didn't say why, but asked me to come back the next day and go to lunch with her.

The next day, I met her outside the little shop and we walked to the restaurant together. She told me she wasn't even supposed to be at the shop the day before, that she should've already left by the time John and I arrived there, and how she felt like she just had to talk to me.

Her son arrived and, after introducing us, she asked him to tell me what God had called him to do. His face lit up as he began to tell me that God had told him to walk across the United States calling people to repent and turn back to God!

What a God appointment that was! I told him about John and I and he was so excited I didn't think he was going to be able to stay in his seat. I can't imagine *walking*. I was very thankful God had provided not only transportation for us, but a home as well. But this young man was only 19 and in good shape. He was so excited about what God had called him to, and I'm sure he is reaching people that we couldn't.

We drove into town to the post office the next day, and I felt led to go back into the coffee shop where we had lunch the day before. As I was waiting inside the door for the Holy Spirit to show me what I was doing in there, I saw him sitting at a table near the back. I knew that's why I had come. As I walked toward that young man, the Lord gave me a word for him. He was very encouraged by it, and I watched his face light up once again.

We never saw him again. Maybe when we get to heaven, God will connect us so we can share stories of our journeys.

The morning we left that campground, we drove around Oklahoma City through the country intending to get on I-40 somewhere near the west side of the city, but God had other plans. The ramp was closed and we were unable to get on the interstate. We had to make a U-turn and follow the signs to get to another on-ramp.

John was calm and I was frustrated. He drove on through traffic and stoplights, finally coming to the sign with an arrow pointing left to I-40.

As soon as we turned, I looked to my right and saw what appeared to be an old motel that had been turned into a residential care home. I could just feel the sadness coming from that place! I tried to get John to look at the building but, of course, he was busy trying to drive.

The Lord spoke to me as we passed by.

You need to go there.

That's all He said, but I immediately told John and he made another one of those U-turns that he was getting quite good at. We parked next door and headed over. John asked me what we were going to do once we got inside. I had no idea, but had grabbed my Chaplain's badge to give us a little credibility.

We were shown into the director's office where we introduced ourselves, told the lady we were in ministry, and asked if we could come in to pray for the residents and give Bibles to whoever would like to have one. She seemed surprised and thrilled that we had Bibles to give away and gave us permission.

We hurried back to the motor home to get some Bibles. I was picking them out of a box where we had all kinds of nice new Bibles. Study Bibles, Devotional Bibles, Bibles for men, women, and children. The Holy Spirit was clearly telling me which Bibles to choose. He kept leading me to a little green Gideon's New Testament and I kept putting it aside to choose what I thought was a bigger, nicer Bible. I finally took that little green one and put it on top of the stack John was trying to hold. I told him I thought that was enough and we headed back, totally unaware we had twenty Bibles and that there were twenty men housed in the halfway house.

The director had gathered the men in the dining room and she told them we were there to pray with them and give out Bibles if they wanted one. The first man who came to my side of the table picked up that little green Gideon's New Testament.

"Could I have this one?" he asked.

I told him he could have any Bible he wanted.

"Oh, I want this one," he said. "You see, I had one just like this when I was nine years old and it went missing. I didn't ever think I'd have another one!"

He continued to tell me with tears in his eyes how, in the front of that little Bible he was clutching to his chest, it told you where to look if you were sick or afraid or lonely. And all I could think was that I almost didn't bring that one. Had the Holy Spirit not kept after me, that one would have still been in the motor home.

John and I prayed with those men for everything from salvation, to healing, to deliverance. For their families and unsaved loved ones. And some asked for prayer that God would help them to stay clean and straight once they got out of there.

Two hours later, we were walking back to where we had parked. The wind was blowing fiercely, blowing my tears back to the sides of my face.

"This is where it's at, John," I said.

What if my husband would have been
tired of making U-turns
by the time I asked him to go back there?
What if I would have allowed
my frustration over the detour
to hinder me from being sensitive
to the Holy Spirit?
There are so many "what ifs"
in our lives.
What if all the people of God
acted like people of God?
And what if...
we were all obedient to do His bidding
as much as is humanly possible?
What a different world it would be!

Amarillo, Texas

It was a Sunday morning in Amarillo, Texas. We had driven around the day before, asking the Lord where we should attend church the next day. We try to attend worship services on Sunday morning and night and even Wednesday evenings if we can find a service nearby. We are not choosy about what kind of church it is. John and I pray and let the Lord lead us to the place He would have us to go. This particular Sunday, He had directed us to a little Baptist church just a couple of blocks from the campground.

After Sunday School, the pastor came back to speak with us. John gave him a prayer card and said, "We are calling America back to God."

Everyone welcomed us warmly. After singing a few songs, the pastor took out the prayer card, put on his glasses to read it out loud, and told the congregation who we were and what our ministry was about. He went on to tell them he knew God had sent us there and how honored they should be for God to entrust them with His special servants. Then the pastor continued by saying they were going to take up an offering for us!

We were shocked! They didn't know us at all, but obviously, God had spoken to that pastor and he wasn't about to be disobedient! What a beautiful surprise and blessing.

We were invited to have lunch with them afterwards, and then we got back on the road.

I once heard a message preached about how
the enemy tries to steal our blessings
as soon as we receive them.
Whether it's a great sermon we've heard,
a gift from a friend,
or anything God has blessed us with.
Immediately, Satan comes to snatch
those blessings,
if we allow him to.
John and I were getting ready
to experience that very thing.

John and I left that church with our hearts filled with the goodness of the Lord, and how that pastor and the congregation had blessed us.

We had only driven about five miles when I noticed a faint odor. It smelled like something electrical was burning. I told John right away. He was unable to smell it, but pulled off the road as soon as he could.

The odor wasn't totally unfamiliar to us. A few months prior, we had noticed the same odor and smoke had actually come out of the air conditioning vents. We had it checked at three different places. They all thought wires had melted together, but no one really knew how to fix it. They just suggested we not use the dash air conditioning. We could start the generator and use the roof air conditioning if we needed it. Most of that summer we traveled without air, and it was a very hot summer. It wasn't always comfortable, but at least the motor home didn't catch on fire.

Now, here we were in Texas, having not even touched the dash buttons, but the odor was unmistakable. And it was getting stronger.

John jumped out to get his tools. I had been breathing a little prayer, but all of a sudden I got angry. By the time John had come back inside, I told him we weren't going to put up with this! He looked at me rather strangely, but quickly understood as I laid my hand on those air conditioning vents and told the enemy to get his hands off this motor home in the name of Jesus! I continued to tell Satan that he wasn't going to steal our blessing from that church and he wasn't going to call a halt to this journey! Then we asked the Lord to cover and protect us and the motor home, got back in our seats, and back on the road. We didn't *ever* smell the burning wires again!

I believe instead of standing strong
in the power and authority
we have in Jesus' name,
we often just cave in
to the enemy.

What do you have need of today, my friend?
Stand up and speak out in the name of Jesus!
And believe He will move mountains for you!

Whatsoever you ask in My name,
that will I do,
so that the Father may be glorified in the Son.
If you ask Me
anything
in My name,
I will do it.

John 14:13-14 (NASB)

A Word for New Mexico

That Sunday evening, we arrived in Tucumcari, New Mexico, and stopped at a small campground to get a spot for the night. The campground was worse than scary. I wanted to turn around and get out of there, but felt the Lord was telling us it would be okay. While John hooked everything up in the camping spot, I got online to find a church. We were hoping to find a place that had Sunday night worship services so we could join them. After a good bit of searching, I was unable to find a single church with a service on Sunday night. Finally, I found a phone number for some kind of ministry and called them.

A nice man answered the phone and, when he found out what I wanted, told me they didn't actually have services there, but that he and his wife usually attended a little Spanish Baptist Church on Sunday evening, and we would be welcome to come. He gave me the address and time of service and said he would look for us there.

John and I got ready, asked the Lord to protect our motor home and our dog while we were gone, and drove the ten minutes or so to the church.

True to his word, the man I had spoken with was standing outside waiting for us. He took us in and introduced us to the pastor, who was a tall, young man from Argentina. We gave him a prayer card and chatted with him a few moments before the service began.

It was a great service! A little unusual, but really good. The message was centered around ladies. The pastor called all the women up front and prayed a blessing over us at the end.

After church, I gave the pastor a copy of my book. The gentleman who had met us there invited us to stop by his ministry the next morning for a tour. We agreed to come around nine o'clock and headed back to the campground.

All was in order when John and I arrived back at the motor home. We were ready to call it a night. John fell asleep almost immediately, but I couldn't get to sleep. I went back over in my mind to see if there was something I needed to do. I had prayed protection over everything. There was nothing else I could think of. Then the Lord spoke to me —

**You need to pray over the land
you are parked on.**

Well, I hadn't thought of that! So I quickly prayed and went right to sleep.

I woke up from a dream. Feeling unsettled and sick to my stomach, I woke John up and asked him to pray for me. We both prayed for a little while. The presence of the Holy Spirit was very evident; soon I saw a vision. It was a silhouette of people standing side by side holding hands. Their feet were spread apart and their arms were stretched out as though to reach the hand of the person next to them.

Do any of you remember those little paper dolls? My mother used to cut those out for me when I was little. She would make a few cuts, pull them apart, and then voilà, all the paper dolls would stretch out, attached by their hands and feet.

I knew those people were praying, but that was all I knew. Then the Lord began to speak to me.

> **If they will pray in earnest,**
> **repent for their state and their nation,**
> **and ask Me to cover their state, I will.**
> **I will protect them.**
> **But they must come to Me with**
> **clean hands, and a clean, sincere heart.**

Even though the Lord hadn't said it specifically, I knew this was a word for New Mexico, probably for the pastors. As I prayed, God revealed more about that word to me.

If the pastors would pray in Tucumcari, Albuquerque, and Gallup, it would be as though they were joined together all the way across the state from east to west, covering their state in prayer.

I thought about the atlas I had looked at earlier, as we were traveling. Tucumcari was the first city on the east side of the state, Albuquerque was in the middle, and Gallup was on the far west side. They were all right on interstate 40.

I was excited! What an amazing word! I could hardly wait to share it the next morning.

After writing the word down, and giving praise and thanksgiving to God for this word from Him, I went back to sleep.

I had two more dreams before morning. After the second one, I got up to pray.

The Lord began to speak to me.

> **If no one offers you a place**
> **to park the motor home,**
> **you are to move on.**

I had already known we were only to stay at that campground one night, but all I could think about was that word from the Lord.

But God, what about giving the pastors the word and sharing the vision with them?

**If no one offers, move on, My child.
Move on today.**

Okay, Lord. Speak to them.

John and I pulled out of the campground on our way to take a tour of the ministry we had been invited to the night before. We parked in an empty parking lot across the street and the man met us at the door.

For about an hour, he showed us all around, seeming to not leave out a single detail. It was obvious he was proud of the ministry. As he talked, it came to me that he worked with most of the pastors in town and that I should ask him about where we could park the motor home.

Finally, it appeared he was coming to a close of talking about the ministry, so I told him about the word from the Lord and then what God had spoken to me this morning in reference to a place to park the motor home. His entire demeanor changed. I felt grief well up inside and was afraid I might actually cry. I explained to him that we would only need to stay a day or two. He told us he really had no ideas, and that if we wanted to, we could just stay parked in the parking lot where we were, and take our chances that we would not be towed because the lot belonged to the city. John and I knew that wasn't the answer. We thanked him and left.

As we walked back toward the motor home, John took my hand. He knew my heart was breaking. I couldn't believe that word would fall to the ground because of this one man! However, I wasn't feeling any liberty to drive around and ask pastors for a place to stay. Besides, God had said —

If no one offers...

*I believe far too often
we only take what we want to hear
out of what God says to us
and cast the remaining
part aside.*

That can be very dangerous.
We need to exercise caution
when we receive a word
from the Lord.
Being careful to go over
every word,
because to leave out
a single word could change the meaning
entirely.

John and I sat in the motor home and prayed. I wept. Surely, there was someone. Surely...

Finally, John reached over and touched my hand. Without him saying a word I knew we had to go. We were heading to Albuquerque and I prayed and cried almost the entire way! The farther away we got, the more I kept asking God if there was some way the pastors in Tucumcari could get that word.

And then my cell phone rang. An unusual voice was at the other end. It was the Spanish Baptist Pastor. He said he had wanted to meet with us but had been busy all day. I told him we were almost to Albuquerque, actually pulling into the campground just then. He was so sorry to have missed us. Then I heard the Lord say —

Give him the word.

God didn't have to tell me twice! I was thrilled!

Unsure of how the pastor would react, I said to him, "I don't know what your beliefs are about God speaking to people, but I need to give you a word from the Lord."

He was silent for a moment before he spoke.

"Miss Maxie," he said, "I believe God can do anything He wants anytime He wants."

He asked me to wait a minute so he could pull over to write it down.

Praise Jesus! He was going to receive it! And he was even sincere enough to want to write it down.

I shared with him the vision and the word from the Lord. He was silent for so long I thought I had lost him.

Then he spoke, "I am honored to be allowed to receive this word. I will take it to the prayer meeting with the pastors on Friday."

Thank You, Lord, for this pastor's heart.

We talked a little more and then he asked if we could pray together before getting off the phone and offered for me to pray first. He was so humble as he prayed, asking God to help him to be brave enough to do what God wanted him to.

I'm sure God knew that word
would fall to this pastor
before He ever gave it to me.

What I don't know is...
how it would have turned out
had we continued to look
for a place to park the motor home
in Tucumcari,
or tried to find a pastor
on our own
to share that word with.

Despite our grief at leaving
Tucumcari without passing on
the word from the Lord,
God used our obedience
to bring redemption
through His perfect will.

After taking a couple of days to rest, we knew it was time to take that word to the pastors in Albuquerque. We asked the Lord to show us where to go. The first church was huge. It looked more like a fancy mall than a church. There was a shiny metal circular staircase to the church office. I barely made it up and wasn't looking forward to coming back down. There must have been an elevator, but I had looked around and couldn't locate one.

A sweet girl greeted me in the office. She told me the pastors were in a staff meeting. (Sometimes I wonder if some pastors spend more time in staff meetings than they do talking to people about the Lord.) I gave her a prayer card with our name and number on it and just said we'd like to speak with your pastor for a few minutes. She told me they would call when the staff meeting was over. It must still be going on...

The next church was one of those where one simply cannot find the office. I'm not sure if some churches are designed like that on purpose or not, but sometimes it seems that way. I just don't think some of those offices could be that hard to locate unless it was intentional.

I went inside to find a lady in a wheelchair with an injured foot propped up. I asked if the pastor was in.

She said, "No."

I asked if she knew when he would be in. She said she had no idea. I thanked her and left.

Feeling a bit frustrated, I walked back to the car, and we got back on the road. We were rounding a curve when John said, "Oh, there's Hobby Lobby."

And God said —

Pull in.

I told John to pull in and, just when we turned into the parking lot, God spoke to me again.

**Go in and give the word
to the manager.**

John gave me a strange look when I told him what the Lord had said, but he didn't say a word. He just got out of the car and walked toward the store with me, holding the door open like he always does.

I asked an employee if there was a manager in the store. She called him for me right away. We stepped over to the side, out of the aisle and, after introducing ourselves and telling him we were traveling across the country calling America back to God, I shared the vision with him and the word from the Lord.

I told him the word needed to get to some pastors who would pray.

He said, "Well, I don't know about pastors, but I can get it to some *praying people.*"

Oh, thank You, Lord, that you always know exactly where to send us and who to send us to.

We thanked him and left. As soon as we got to the car, the Lord spoke to me.

That's it. It's time to move on.

What? I couldn't believe it. No more churches or pastors in a city the size of Albuquerque? I guess not. The torch had been passed.

Gallup

The next morning, we headed west. Toward Gallup. John had picked up a booklet about the town. Every time I picked up that booklet, it fell open to a campground. The same campground every time. The picture looked like it might be a little pricey. I finally told the Lord if He wanted us to stop there, He was going to have to tell me. Almost no sooner were the words out of my mouth when He answered me.

I want you to stay there for one week.

But God, we can't afford to stay an entire week.

**Tell the owner what you and John
are doing and I'll take care of the rest.**

We found a nice man behind the counter when we went in. He was tall and had on bifocals. We told him we wanted to stay a week, then I asked if they ever gave discounts to people in full-time ministry.

He looked at me over the top of his glasses and said, "No."

I said, "Oh. Okay." But I'm thinking, "Okay God, now what?"

John is giving the man information and he's filling out the form.

Then he looked up again and asked, "What kind of ministry?"

"We're traveling across the country calling America back to God."

He responded, "We sure need that!"

He returned to his writing. He looked back up and told us he could come down to such and such. We thanked him. It wasn't much, maybe 10%, but better than nothing.

Then he looked at me and asked if we were giving a presentation somewhere. I told him we weren't, but that we planned to speak to some pastors. He peered at me over those glasses again.

"Well, maybe I could come down to such and such."

That would have been about a 25% discount, I think. We thanked him again.

He was just about finished with the form when he stood up straight and looked at me one more time.

"If you can pay cash, I'll give you 50% off for the whole week."

We couldn't believe it! After thanking him profusely, we paid the bill and went back out to drive to what would be our home for the next week.

"What just happened in there?" John asked.

"I'm not sure, but I know God showed up."

The Holy Spirit was sure speaking to that man! And he was listening. We hadn't even argued with him when he offered the first discount to us! But that obviously wasn't the discount God intended for us to have.

We spoke to that man a number of times during our stay there and he was always very nice. He went out of his way to help the campers however he could.

This would be the longest we had stayed anywhere on this trip. We were thankful it was such a nice campground.

The date was November 1st, 2012.
Just five days before the
2012 Presidential Election.

Feeling it was of great importance,
I had been praying for weeks
about where God would have us to be
during the election.
It appeared He wanted us
in Gallup, New Mexico.
November 6th would also be a year
since God had told me I had one
year to call them to repent.
I don't understand that word
now a whole lot more
than I did then,
although I have some ideas.

We had no idea, however,
what God would allow
us to see during
the week we spent in Gallup.

John parked the motor home and was hooking up when I decided to take advantage of the free Wi-Fi and check some things online. I had only been connected for five minutes or so when I got kicked offline. After trying unsuccessfully to get back on a couple of times, I gave up and picked up my phone to text our daughter to let her know where we would be for the next week. That was when things began to get strange.

The screen on my cell phone read *"Unable to determine your time zone."*

What on earth? I had never seen that on my phone! And to top it all off we weren't even close to a time zone change! We had crisscrossed them a number of times on our journey, but my phone didn't do anything except automatically change the time.

I asked John to come in and showed him my phone. He looked at his flip phone. It didn't have anything unusual on it but showed he had no service. That wasn't really out of the ordinary. Our cell provider wasn't known for having the best coverage, but we had been with them for years and had just learned to live with it.

By this time, the message about the time zone was off my phone, and I didn't have any service either.

My stomach began to churn. Deep inside I felt something wasn't right but had no idea what it could be. I tried to ignore that feeling as we drove to the grocery store.

As we walked through the doors at the store, a cashier called out, "No cards! Just cash!"

We didn't pay much attention and went on through the store to do our shopping. After paying cash for our groceries, we got into the car and went back to the campground. I had looked at my phone in the parking lot at the store to see if I had service there, but no luck.

During supper, and the cleaning up afterwards, John noticed I was unusually quiet. He knew I was really upset about the cell phones although we hadn't talked much about it. He also knew I had sensed something wasn't right. Deep inside, I knew this wasn't a normal lack of cell phone or Wi-Fi service. It went far beyond that. I had been praying on and off as we went about our normal activities. Finally, John suggested we go for a drive to see if we could get into an area where we had phone service. Then I could at least let our daughter know where we were. She has kept up with us every night since this journey began, keeping track of exactly where we stop every night. John knew that was part of why I was distraught, but he knew it was far more than that. He had seen God move time and time again when I had a strong sense about something. He had no intention of ignoring how I felt.

I agreed to go, but insisted we take Moses with us. We normally leave him in the motor home when we go out, but I wasn't even comfortable leaving our dog behind that night.

As I walked out of the motor home and down the steps, I turned around, looked at John and said, "This is a trial run by the government."

I'm not sure why I said that.
It just seemed to come right out
of my mouth.
As far as I know I hadn't been
thinking about that...
And then again, maybe I had.

We stopped at the office before leaving the campground to see if they knew anything. They didn't seem to be concerned, just attributing it to a car that had hit a cell tower or something. Their complacency didn't make me feel any better.

A few miles down the main road we found a hotel. John went inside to speak with the lady behind the desk. He came back to the car with more information than either of us had wanted to know. According to the desk clerk, not only did they not have internet or cell phone service (with any provider), they didn't have landline service either. She told my husband they couldn't even make a 911 call if they needed to. So far, no one had been able to determine what the problem was.

After digesting that, I thought we should drive back toward the interstate to the Travel Center. After all, truck drivers know *everything.*

John pulled up in front of the store and stayed in the car with Moses so he wouldn't bark while I went inside. There was a group of men standing in a circle talking. They seemed to be having a serious conversation and I knew what they were talking about. I kind of scooted in between two of the guys and looked around the circle. They all appeared to be truck drivers except one. He had on a uniform shirt with a patch that read Manager. I asked them if they knew how far this went.

The manager spoke up and said, "As far as I know it goes from Amarillo, Texas, to Phoenix, Arizona, and we are losing $10,000 an hour and it's been four hours! This is more than a downed-tower!"

Wow! I stepped back about half a step to look around. All the way to my left there was a big man standing in front of a pay phone. He was holding the receiver in his left hand and hitting the phone with his right.

He turned all the way around and met my eyes from across the room. It was a little strange. There were dozens of people in there and he kept looking until he saw me.

Then he said directly to me, "This is no downed tower!"

He turned back to the phone, which of course wasn't working.

I continued to gaze around the room, stopping at a lady in front of an ATM machine. She was kicking the machine and cursing it! And just like the pay phone, of course it wasn't going to work either.

I eased back into the circle in time to see one of the truck drivers take a huge roll of bills out of his pocket.

He held the money out to the manager and said, "I just need to get some fuel and get on the road!"

The manager responded with, "You have no idea how bad I wish I could take your money, but the diesel pumps can only be activated by a card. I can take cash for gasoline, but have to have a card for diesel fuel."

I had seen enough. It was pure chaos in there. Everyone was upset, some more than others, and it was escalating. One man thought it was a terrorist attack. I left the store and got in the car with my husband, thankful he was there with me.

As we drove back to the campground, I shared with him everything I had learned.

"We need to pray," he said.

Yes, we certainly did.

After arriving back at the motor home, John went straight to the CB radio to see what he could hear. After going through 23 channels, there was nothing but total silence. We were only about a mile from the interstate. There would certainly have been radio traffic from the truckers if their CBs were working.

I was terribly unsettled in my spirit. I knew part of it was in the natural. We were down to very little cash and, if this situation didn't turn around soon, I wasn't sure how we could travel without cash for gas. For that matter, even if we had cash, it wouldn't take long for all the stations to run out of gasoline if the trucks couldn't get there to bring more in.

Of course, the same is true for everything. I know, in North Carolina, if the weatherman is calling for snow flurries, the bread and milk is gone from the grocery stores within the hour! What if we were unable to get *anything* delivered? We would all be in the same boat, I guess, and it would quickly get to be an uncomfortable boat, but I wasn't thrilled about being all the way over here in New Mexico should any of that happen. Trusting God was the only answer; I knew that. He knew where we were, and He wouldn't have put us in a place without a plan. God had told us specifically to stay in this campground for one week. And this was only our first night here...

John and I prayed until late that night and finally went to bed. I had entered a text message into my phone and sent it to my daughter, having no idea when or even if she would get it.

In the morning, my phone had service and showed the text had gone through around 3:30am. It was 3:15pm when the time zone message had first been on the main screen of my phone. It appeared that communications had been down for approximately twelve hours.

John and I went out to find a newspaper or two so that we could take them with us. We wanted to read what was in the news about the situation we had experienced. We were shocked to find there was nothing! Absolutely nothing! Things were back to normal, so no one seemed to care what had happened. A friend did some research for me and could only find one tiny line buried somewhere about the communications being out in that area.

To this day,
John and I don't know
what really happened.
We have no idea
if that communications blackout
reached as far as the manager
of the travel center
thought it did.

What we do know is,
if that would have taken place
in NYC or Chicago,
or even most any place
more densely populated
than the area we were in,
it would have been a disaster!

Possibly big enough to justify
calling for martial law.

Oh, and we know one more thing...
It took place just five days before the
2012 Presidential Election.

Divine Appointments

Things were definitely looking up today. Not only were communications restored, but the pastor from Tucumcari called to say the pastors at the meeting were greatly receptive to the word from the Lord. That was balm to my ears! I shared with him about the manager at Hobby Lobby, and he asked for his name so he could talk with him. He also gave me a pastor's name in Gallup that we could talk to. It was wonderful to see that fruit was beginning to grow because of the word God had given.

John and I headed out to speak to pastors, asking God to direct us all along the way. The pastor who had been referred to us was out of state and wouldn't be back for a few days. We were unable to connect with any others. God was allowing us to get a good feel for the area, but we obviously hadn't located the one God had chosen for us to pass the torch to.

We had seen signs about a flea market. I'm not usually a fan of those. Now a good yard sale would be great, but flea markets don't hold much interest for me. However, I was feeling drawn to this one so, after making some inquiries, we drove to the edge of town the next morning and located it.

This flea market was huge! There were cars parked on both sides of the road for a long way before we could even see it. God had definitely gone before us! A pickup truck backed out from the closest parking spot to the entrance and we pulled in.

A few people always ask me,
"Do you really pray for parking places?"
Of course I do!
(Especially if it's raining.)
God can either provide one or not...
however He chooses.
But I have found that if I ask,
He usually provides the perfect spot.

This flea market was unlike anything I had ever seen. One of the first things we noticed were some unusual looking pigs for sale, and it went on from there.

This area of the country is home to many Native Americans. I believe most of the booths belonged to them and they had some really great stuff; clothing, blankets, jewelry, and lots of good food. One could also find car parts, hay bales, appliances, and all kinds of smaller farm animals. What I found most interesting were the Medicine Man booths. All their wares were laid out carefully in glass bowls or some other orderly way, and they were eager to tell you about each item. Some even offering us (encouraging us really) to try them out. There were powders to calm you, to help your headaches, to make you "see" better; something for just about any ailment one might have. We declined their offers to try anything and just walked and looked, stopping to chat with people here and there. We were trying to be sensitive to the Holy Spirit, not wanting to miss anything God might be showing us.

A little later in the day, I felt we should go to the little downtown area. Often, John and I feel led to a particular area where we will walk or drive, and pray. Sometimes God just wants us to pray over a certain place, and other times He shows us something particular or has a divine appointment set up for us. This was to be the day of a huge divine appointment. One we certainly would not have wanted to miss!

John and I walked slowly, praying quietly as we went. It wasn't long before I felt a strong tug toward a little shop. It was a co-op where four or five people took turns manning the store and all their things were displayed for sale. Everything was beautiful! It could have been an art museum.

As we looked around, the lady behind the counter started chatting with us. She was a little out of breath from rushing to get there. She had come straight from the flea market and began to tell John about the great parking place God had given her. That caught my attention and I dragged my gaze away from the lovely pottery I was looking at to the lady behind the counter. This was a God set-up. I'm pretty familiar with those by now and I usually recognize one pretty quickly.

I walked over to the counter and we began to talk. It seemed all three of us recognized it at the same time and we jumped right in, not wanting to waste time on small talk. John and I shared about our ministry and the call God had on our lives, while she shared her story.

She and her husband had lived in Kansas when God spoke to them about a journey not unlike ours. God was telling them to divest themselves of everything, including their home; get an RV and go to Gallup, New Mexico. That was four years ago.

"So are you still living in your RV?" I asked.

"Yes. We are parked at USA RV Park," she told me.

I couldn't believe it! That's the same place we were. No one but God could have orchestrated all this.

She was really excited about the word God had given me for New Mexico when I shared it with her. She felt certain her pastor would meet with us to hear the word.

God had brought her husband to Gallup to head up the building of a church. It was the same church I had read about in a brochure and showed to John, telling him I had a strong feeling about it, but needed to pray more about what God was showing me.

The lady told us about all the red tape they had to cut through, and the spiritual warfare that took place over the building of that

115

church. The enemy definitely did not want that church to be built! Today, a number of Native American tribes are represented in that spirit-filled church.

She and her husband make pottery when they aren't ministering to the Native American people. Their things are beautiful. Wanting to bless us, she insisted we choose a piece to take with us. I looked at everything for a long while, going from one piece to the next. I felt this was a Holy Spirit moment as well, and I didn't want to get something just because it was unique and beautiful. I wanted to get the very thing God had for us in that shop.

Finally, after showing it to John, I chose a small whistle. As my new friend carefully wrapped it in paper and tucked it inside a small white bag, she told us the story of the whistle.

It wasn't really supposed to be a whistle, you see. She had been invited to speak to a group of school children about making pottery. As she held this small piece of clay in her hands, she began to work with it and form it. While she worked, she compared the lump of clay to each of us until we accept Jesus. Then He molds us and makes each one of us into the person we are meant to be. She looked down at the clay in her hands, wondering what she could turn it into that would appeal to the children. Then she saw a whistle. Not a whistle that we would recognize. This one was pointed at both ends, almost like a little closed-in canoe. It had a couple of little slits she had poked into it and she made a place to blow into.

Let's see, she thought, if this will work. If it didn't, she needed an idea fast because she felt the children needed to see that lump of clay turn into something they could relate to.

Sure enough. It blew clear and loud. There was an unusual sound to it. After blowing it a few times, she almost felt like the Holy Spirit had been ushered in. It kind of reminded her of blowing the shofar.

A number of those children prayed with her that day to ask Jesus into their hearts. God was definitely the One fashioning that whistle.

It felt like we both knew a short amount of time had been allotted to us, and she needed to impart a certain amount of information to me in that time frame. We covered a lot of territory, more than would be possible in the natural it seemed.

After arranging to meet at their church the following morning, John and I hugged our new friend and said our goodbyes.

Stepping out of that little store,
we felt as though we had just come
out of a supernatural place
back into the real world.
It was almost like a jolt to us.
And even though we hadn't noticed
it earlier,
now it felt rather harsh out here.

Always an early bird, John and I arrived at church before our friends. The pastor greeted us and said he had received a phone call the night before to let him know we would be coming. He asked if we had time to give him the word now, before church started. The timing wouldn't have been my choice; I felt he might be distracted knowing church would begin soon, but I was thankful he wanted to hear the word.

We learned that this was actually the assistant pastor; the senior pastor was out of town. He invited the missionary who was scheduled to speak that day to come into the room with us while I shared the vision God had given me and the word from the Lord for New Mexico.

I'm not sure if the pastor said anything. The missionary spoke to John.

"So she's the speaker and you're the armor-bearer?"

John just put his arm around me and smiled.

117

It had been twelve minutes since we had walked into the room and it was still thirty minutes before the service was to begin.

The pastor jumped up and ran out of the room, saying something about "having to get back out there." The missionary thanked us and we went out together. The pastor didn't speak to us again.

I found the missionary's message especially interesting. I think you will too, so I'm going to briefly share a few of his points.

His message came from 2 Chronicles 14 and 15.

1. A prayer to heal our land
2. The purpose of a word from God is to find you and redirect your life.
3. A word from God begins not with the prophet- but with God.
4. Sometimes the word you need...is when you think you don't need it.

There was of course a lot more to the message than this, but these were some of the major points.

I felt some disappointment
creeping in because of
the response from the pastor.
You would think by now
I would be past that.
But I'm not sure
if that actually ever comes.

The urgency of this call
and the knowing that our nation
is one step away from
judgment
brings me to a place
where I sometimes want
to make people understand.
And yet I also know
understanding will come
only through the Holy Spirit.

I am just the messenger.

Our new friends took us out for lunch after church. We spent a wonderful two hours sharing. The following day, I rode my bike to their RV, which was just a short ride down the road from where our camping spot was. I went inside to find my friend canning jam. She immediately made some hot tea for us and sat down to visit.

> *God is so good!*
> *He knew how badly I needed a friend*
> *and this friend knew exactly*
> *how I was feeling*
> *because she had been there;*
> *Was even still there*
> *to some extent.*
> *I don't ever run out of*
> *amazement*
> *at the things God does*
> *for us.*

Our new friends wanted to take us to dinner the following night because they felt there was a couple who needed to meet us. That would be Tuesday, November 6th, Election Day.

But he who listens to me
shall live securely
and will be at ease
from the dread of evil.

Proverbs 1:33 (NASB)

November 6th, 2012

The Dream

It was 1:19am when I awoke. I got up to pray, especially for my son this morning. We pray for our children every day, but he was especially on my heart today as this is his birthday.

I went back to sleep after a while and then woke up from a dream. I jotted down some notes so I wouldn't forget, intending to write the entire dream down in my journal later. There would be no chance of not remembering the dream, however. I went back to sleep and woke up from the same exact dream three more times.

I have had instances where I will dream the same thing or something very similar two or three times in one night, but I don't ever remember having the exact same dream four times. The dreams were identical. They started at the same place and ended the same with all the same details. God definitely wanted me to get ahold of this dream.

The dream began with me standing in the middle of a road looking at an old, old grey stone house that was on fire. It had obviously been burning for a while because there was only about two feet left standing on two of the walls, and the other two walls were almost completely gone. There didn't seem to be anything left inside at all.

121

The house was at the end of the road. The road just ended and the stone house sat there with only a few feet of grass in front of it. There were no other structures around it, only land and trees.

To my left stood what was left of a red brick house. It was almost completely burned down as well. Both houses were still burning a little, but most of the fire was out. I couldn't see any other houses or buildings. It seems there were houses on both sides of the road as I walked to the end, but the dream actually began at the end of the road, so I'm not sure why I would think there were other houses.

The stone house had been large, but not overly so. The red brick house had been tall and stately, possibly with columns in front. The stone house was very old. The brick house was not new, but much newer than the stone one. I don't know exactly how I knew these things; I just did.

It was dusk when I first came to the end of that road. As I stood looking at the scene in front of me and to my right, night settled in.

I finally noticed the firefighters. There were only a few and they looked rather dejected. Sad almost, like they had given up. I blinked, trying to see them better through the dark, smoky air. They looked odd to me. I realized they looked like they had come out of an old movie, or better yet, an old picture. Their uniforms appeared to be very old and out of date.

They were walking around slowly with their heads hung down and shoulders drooping. The air was dark and smoky causing me to hardly be able to see them.

It's strange. I don't recall seeing a fire truck or any type of vehicle. I did, however, notice some old looking hoses that they must have been using to fight the fire.

My eyes kept going back to the old stone house. I was wondering how those stones could have just burned? And even the brick? If the houses were made of wood, I could understand. The stones and bricks seemed to have just disintegrated.

I kept looking into the darkness, trying to "see" something. I felt there was something I needed to see. I looked a little to my right and way off in the distance. I could see some buildings that looked like a city. I was surprised to see flames shooting up from some of those buildings. But my eyes continued to be drawn back to the old stone house.

I finally took a couple of steps forward, moving a little closer. A couple of the firefighters sprang into action, running toward me.

"The only way to go is back the way you came. There is only fire, darkness, and danger up ahead. You MUST go back the way you came!" they said.

I didn't speak but stopped moving forward. That seemed to satisfy them and they went back to hanging their heads down, moving about slowly in the side yard to the left of the stone house.

As I looked to the right again, off in the distance, it was very dark. The last flames had died out. It was smoky, but it seemed I could see a few scattered shapes that appeared to be floating around near the tops of the buildings. They obviously hadn't burned almost to the ground like the houses near me.

I was drawn back to that old stone house. I carefully stepped a little closer to the end of that road. Immediately the firefighters came toward me, one of them acting as though he wanted to push me back the other way, the way I had come, to keep me safe.

"You MUST turn back! There is only destruction up ahead! You must go back the way you came!"

After dreaming this four times in one night, I was unable to think of much else by the time I got up.

"God," I asked, "what is this about?"

As I talked to the Lord about the dream, I felt it was about our nation. How we *must* turn back to our Bible-based values. Turn back to when right was right and wrong was wrong. Turn back to when, as a nation, we had a holy fear of God and a respect for Him and the Bible.

But there was also an inkling somewhere inside of me wondering if there was a personal interpretation to this dream. Were John and I supposed to turn back?

Three close friends called that morning checking up on us, and I shared the dream with each of them. One said we needed to turn back immediately! Another said we needed to pray about it, but possibly God was saying we should turn back. And the third friend didn't feel we should turn back at all.

I can just imagine many of you
smiling at this
...as I am.
I wouldn't have shared the dream
with just anyone.
But all three of these ladies
are close friends,
confidantes,
two of them are even on our
ministry team today.
Wise, Godly counsel is wonderful!
And I am so thankful for their input.
But the bottom line is,
after acquiring that counsel,
we must each seek our own answer
from the Lord.

The Round Church with the Stars

That evening, our new friends drove down the street and picked us up to go to dinner. We went to a great little local place right off the downtown area. The other couple arrived and the six of us squeezed into a round corner booth. It was a table arrangement you normally would be uncomfortable with, especially with people you didn't know, but we were pleased with our table. We all leaned in and put our heads together from

124

time to time. It felt sort of like a private summit. And I believe that's what it was.

We had barely sat down when the new guy said, "So we want to hear your story."

I laughed. Then looked him in the eye and asked, "How long do you have?"

He didn't bat an eye, "As long as it takes."

And he meant it. He recognized the importance of this meeting.

So John and I talked. We stopped long enough to order and then continued to talk. No one interrupted us and no one seemed bored or uneasy. When the food came it was delicious. We took turns talking and eating.

We told our story, pretty much from the beginning. Then we all talked about the communications blackout. They, like us, had never experienced anything like that before. I shared the dream. They were all quiet, reverent almost...and no one had an opinion.

Finally, I knew I needed to share the vision and word from the Lord. I had been putting it off because, when it came to my mind, I found I was close to tears. We would leave in 36 hours and I didn't feel anyone had truly "heard" that word yet.

Sure enough, the tears came as I began to share that word. I finally got it all out and they were all respectfully quiet again. The man we had just met that evening, who had asked to hear our story, began to speak.

"Miss Maxie," he said, "your heart is grieving because you haven't yet been able to pass that word to someone in Gallup. Is that right?"

"Yes. Yes, that's exactly right."

He continued, "You didn't know I was a pastor, did you?"

I could only shake my head.

"I pastor the homeless people in and around Gallup. They call me the pastor of the *Round Church with the Stars.* I receive that word from the Lord and, believe me, my people know how to pray!"

*Tears are running down my face
even now as I write this.
Some of you may wonder
what all the fuss is about.
Why the tears?*

*If you have never received
a word or mandate from the Lord
and the urgency and burden
which comes along with that,
you may not understand my tears.
That's all right.
Just suffice it to say
"The torch had been passed."*

*We arrived back at the motor home
to find our country had re-elected
Barack Obama
to his second term
as President of the United States.*

Continuing On

Wednesday morning found John and I finishing laundry and getting the motor home ready to leave the following morning. We had not heard a clear word from God that we were to turn back, so we would continue heading west. We truly felt God would have told us clearly if there was danger ahead and if we were not to stay the course.

Our friends called again, wanting to take us to dinner one last time to another local place they thought we would enjoy. This restaurant was bigger and fancier. The conversation was more lighthearted. It was as though they knew we needed to leave on a lighter note.

Native Americans came through the restaurant with jewelry and other items. They would stop at the tables to see if the customers wanted to purchase something. A girl brought some pretty fuzzy house slippers to our table with Indian designs on them. My friend asked if they were my size and bought them for me. I wear them often and think of her and our time in Gallup.

When we said our goodbyes, both couples made donations to the ministry, and our friends from the campground gave us homemade jam, Indian jewelry, and a beautiful Navajo Indian blanket.

We will never forget those people and our time in Gallup. What a blessing they had all turned out to be. We couldn't thank God enough for them. John and I both needed the fellowship and friendship of these great people. Leaving our family, friends, and church behind hasn't been easy, but we wouldn't trade anything to follow where God is leading us.

Kingman, Arizona

We woke up to the sun streaming through the windshield all the way through to the back of the motor home. With it came hope and joy renewed! We would continue to head west one day at a time. We would listen carefully to what the Lord was saying and turn back at any point if He told us to.

We drove almost all the way through Arizona. We were a little surprised God hadn't told us to stop anywhere, but we just kept rolling. Finally, we stopped to spend the night in a Walmart parking lot in Kingman, Arizona. We were 51 miles from the California state line and planned to go on into California the next morning.

At 1:13am Friday morning, I woke up to a fierce wind. It was loud and the motor home was rocking a bit, but I had such a sense of peace. I lay there a few minutes and then I heard the song again.

>**The storm is coming.**
>**The storm is coming.**
>**It will wipe the land clean.**
>**Wipe the land clean.**

Maybe it was because I could hear the wind howling, but the storm seemed close. Closer, nearer than before. I heard the Lord again.

>**Just as you hear the wind blowing, My child,**
>**My Holy Spirit is doing a work**
>**in the hearts of people.**

> But it will not become apparent
> until there is much
> persecution and destruction.
>
> Then you will see manifestations
> of My glory as never before.

I prayed and repented for our nation and the people of God for a long while.

When we looked outside later that morning, we could hardly believe it. The parking lot was full of RVs and semi trucks.

There were 70-80 mph winds that lasted all day and into the night. All of those high profile vehicles had to get off the road. There was no way they could cross the mountain passes in that wind.

We could barely even get the motor home door open, so John and I busied ourselves putting together a puzzle, reading, and resting for most of the day. It looked like it would be Saturday before we could go on into California.

But California was not to be. I woke up and immediately heard the Lord say —

> You are not to go into California, My child.
> I have taken My hand off California.

Oh, my! I looked at the clock. It was 2:50am Saturday. I guess we would not be going into California today. I got up to pray.

> You are to give a word, My child.
> A word in Arizona.
> That is why you're here.
>
> The storm is coming!
> Prepare your people.
> Prepare now!
> They must draw near to Me
> or they will not be protected

in the days to come.

**And you will be held accountable
if you do not help your people
prepare for what is coming.**

Fast, pray, and prepare.

When John got up I shared with him what the Lord had said. He was very calm about it and told me he hadn't thought we would be going into California. He had a check in his spirit about it.

Thinking we would leave a little later in the day, John took the motor home to fill up with gas, dump the tanks, and get fresh water; while I took the car around Kingman, praying as I drove. I was expecting God to show me where to stop and, as usual, He didn't disappoint me.

It was a small storefront Catholic Church. I had never seen a storefront Catholic Church before. All the ones I have seen have been large and beautiful. They were having a yard sale out front and a lady told me the Father was in mass, but she was sure he would be happy to talk with me when he got out. It would be about 20 minutes.

Sure enough. Right on time the lady took me in to meet him. He invited me to sit down at a table and listened carefully and respectfully to all I had to say. He got emotional as he told me he knew God had sent me and completely agreed with the word from the Lord.

He had been trying to prepare his people but, he said, "They don't want to hear it. They want to pretend everything is going to be all right, and I don't know what to do to get them to listen."

We talked a little longer and prayed together. After praying he excused himself for a moment and came back with a piece of paper for me. He said God had spoken to him that there was someone I needed to talk to. He had tried to call the man but was unable to reach him.

"Would you go to this church tomorrow morning and speak to this pastor? And tell him I sent you."

I knew it was God. It looked like we wouldn't be leaving Arizona today after all.

God is Still on the Throne

Sunday morning found us with the car already hooked up and the motor home ready to go. We knew exactly where the church was because we had driven the route the day before in the car to make sure it was okay for the motor home. We were planning to leave right after church.

We were early, as usual and, after parking in a spot that we could get out of easily, John and I walked over to the church. I had to stop for a minute to snap a couple of pictures of 15 to 20 jackrabbits in the backyard of a house nearby. They were huge and had super long ears. They looked as big as a medium sized dog!

The pastor and a deacon were standing outside the church talking when we walked up. After introducing ourselves, I knew the Lord was urging me to give that pastor the word right then.

I said to him, "I have a word from the Lord for you."

He backed up a couple of steps and said, "Okay."

I gave him the word about the storm and preparing his people, how he would be held accountable if he didn't prepare them. He just looked at me. I hadn't meant to shock him, but it looked like I had.

I smiled and said, "We'll just head on in to Sunday School."

He followed us inside and showed us to the classroom.

The people were nice, but I don't remember much of what they talked about. As we were exiting the room, I noticed the pastor standing just to the right of the door.

He approached us and said, "Maxie, would you speak to the congregation this morning? I know God sent you and I believe you have a word for our people."

I must have let my surprise show because he said, "Oh dear, I'm afraid I've put you on the spot."

"No. Not at all. I don't really get put on the spot anymore. I'd be happy to."

He thanked me, and we went out to find a seat. I asked John to pray and told him I had no idea what I needed to say, but that God would let me know by the time I stood up to say it. And I knew that He would.

Early on in the service, the pastor told the congregation about John and I and how he had asked me to speak to them because he felt God had given me a word for the people. I stood up to speak and sure enough I knew at least the first part of what I was to tell them. God would give me the rest as I went.

I looked out at those people. I'm not sure how many there were. Maybe 250. They all looked so downcast. I don't know if I saw a smile in the entire group, although I might have missed one. I hadn't noticed it before, but I sure saw it now. The following is what God gave me to tell that congregation.

>You have been very discouraged,
>distraught even,
>over the results of the election.

>If you need to grieve over it,
>do so, but make it brief.

>There is much work to be done
>and not much time to do it.

Our job as people of God hasn't changed!

**And no matter who sits
in the White House,
God is still on the throne!**

Knowing I had done what God sent me there to do, I thanked them and sat down. And the service continued.

At the end of the service, people flocked to John and I. We couldn't even get out of our row. They were standing all the way around us. There was a group of maybe twenty or so who stood off to the side, but otherwise, it appeared the entire congregation had come to speak to us and they were all saying the same thing! They were thanking us for being obedient, for coming to give the word. Telling us how they had been so down, so depressed. Some said they had almost given up on God, thinking if He couldn't handle this election, all hope was lost. And many said they almost didn't come to church this morning.

This was the first Sunday following the election. It appeared God was right on and right on time! Would we have expected any less?

In the middle of all of this a lady squeezed through the crowd to ask us if we would come to her home for lunch the following day. It crossed my mind that we had planned to leave right after church but, once again, I knew this was God. I asked her to write down her address and phone number and give it to John, and told her we would come.

A little later, we pulled away from the church and went back to the Walmart parking lot. Normally, we don't spend more than one night in a row at Walmart, on occasion possibly two. This would make four nights at the same Walmart, but they didn't seem to have a problem with it. They must have been used to it. RVs parked there every day.

The lady had given us directions to her house. It was about five miles outside town. Beautiful scenery was all around us as we drove. We made one turn and it was just a short distance to the entrance to their neighborhood. As we came over a small rise in the road, I gasped. Straight ahead the road simply ended! Just like in my dream. The road was wide and the asphalt just ended and then there was grass and flat land. The houses weren't there, but the end of the road sure was. And in the distance, out in front of me and to my right was a town. It looked similar to the city I had seen in the distance in my dream. I didn't know what to make of all that.

We turned into the neighborhood. There were beautiful southwestern style homes, all different styles and colors. Pulling up in front of the home where we had been invited for lunch, we noticed the lady was watching for us. We got out and went up to the door she was holding open.

Right away, as soon as we got inside, she said, "I need to tell you why I invited you here." She had our attention.

"You see," she said, "a few years ago we got a new pastor. I don't know how much you know about our denomination, but most of our churches don't believe in the gifts of the Holy Spirit. But this pastor and his wife brought the River and many of us jumped in. He taught us about the baptism of the Holy Spirit and speaking in tongues; he taught us about anointing, laying on of hands, and healing. Our church was totally changed. Oh, there were a few who didn't want any part of it, but most of us were so blessed and wanted all we could get. He was here for six wonderful, glorious years."

She sighed long and hard. "And then, four years ago, he was hit by a car while he was out walking. And he was killed. And we haven't had a fresh word from the Lord since then, until you came into our church yesterday morning. And that's why I invited you."

While that was sinking in, she went on to say that she had wanted to invite lots of people today, to meet us and have lunch and talk to us, but wasn't sure if she should, so she had only invited one person. Her very good friend.

"I hope that was okay," she said.

Of course it was okay,
I told her.
I could barely breathe,
much less talk.

What if we hadn't gone
to that church?
What if we had left too soon?
What if I hadn't waited to
speak with the Catholic priest?
What if????

What if we hadn't come today?
We would have never known...
What about the times we may
have missed it?
Not just John and I,
but all of us.
What about the times
you have missed it?

Missed an opportunity
to do something for the Lord.
Something that might have made
the world a much better place
for someone.
Something that could have been
of eternal value.
Missed it because
you or I were tired.
Or didn't have time.
Or thought it might cost us.
Or...because we might look foolish.

What about the times we have just been
disobedient?
What about it?
At least we can repent.

I reached out to that lady and
enveloped her in a big hug.

Of course it was all right
that she had invited her friend.

It would have been all right
had she invited 100 friends.

The lady told us the pastor who is there now is an interim pastor, and a precious man, he just doesn't have an understanding of the moving of the Holy Spirit like their previous pastor.

This also helped to explain the tremendous response John and I had received after the service. Those people were responding to a taste of the River they had been longing for.

I knew those people were grieving what they no longer had. I also felt this interim pastor may be hearing God more than they realized. Otherwise, he probably wouldn't have asked me to say anything at all. It's possible he's just not as comfortable or as experienced in the ways of the Holy Spirit as the pastor they lost.

John and I ate lunch and visited with those people for a number of hours. I'm not even sure how long it was and it doesn't matter. What matters is that we were obedient. And we are trusting God to use the little bit that we can do, for something eternal.

Heading Back

After leaving Kingman, John and I drove about 150 miles and stopped in a Walmart parking lot for the night. The Lord had spoken to us that we were not to go back the way we came, so we were taking a different route.

The following day, we drove almost 500 miles. John had to be exhausted. Driving a big motor home and towing a car takes so much more out of you than just driving a regular vehicle.

We were quiet as we drove. I'm so thankful my husband is so easy to be with. Many people need conversation, or the radio, or something going on all the time. We can ride for miles without saying a word, just smiling at each other now and again. Other times we talk non-stop, sometimes we sing. And sometimes I cry.

During the afternoon that day, I began to cry. I felt such a burden for our nation. I finally just sobbed and sobbed. And my husband just quietly prayed.

I believe this may have been
the first time I had the vision
of the doors.
(I'll talk more about those
later in the book.)
As I wept,
I could "see" these closed doors.

And I knew that people
in high positions,
were making decisions,
very important decisions,
that would affect all of us...
behind those closed doors.

When we stopped for the night, I was exhausted and thankful for my bed. The burden had lifted and I was able to sleep well in another Walmart parking lot.

I should put in a plug here for Walmart. Most Walmarts, all across the country, allow RVers to park in their lots overnight. We try not to take advantage of that by only staying one night (occasionally two) before we head on down the road. Kingman, Arizona, was definitely an exception.

Early on in this journey I noticed delivery vans, other RVs, and sometimes semis would park very close to us. It irritated me a bit. Why was it necessary for them to be two feet from my window? Until one day the Lord spoke to me about this. He told me people felt safe parking near us. Even though most of them didn't understand that it was because of the Holy Spirit, they were drawn to park close to us. After that, I didn't mind waking up and seeing someone parked near our motor home. Most of the time, I pray for those people who are parked there.

One morning, a man in a delivery van had parked close by for the night. He was sitting in the drivers' seat the next morning, reading a book. His window was down and I felt I should go talk to him.

Approaching his window, I said, "Hi!" and asked him what he was reading.

He smiled and turned the book so I could read the cover. I was pleasantly surprised to find it was a good Christian book. We talked a few minutes and, after finding out he loved to read, I brought him a copy of my book with a prayer card. He seemed genuinely pleased and thanked me.

A couple of hours later, John and I were walking back to the motor home with some groceries when he called out to me.

He said, "I'm reading your book and I've looked at your prayer card. I'm so glad I met you and your husband. I believe God wants me to start praying for you guys and your ministry. I wanted you to know I'll be praying for you as I'm traveling. I'm glad I parked next to you."

I was so blessed by this.
We just never know
what God is going to do next.
He moves all of us around
like pieces on a chessboard...
if we will let Him.
And not just any chessboard,
but the Kingdom chessboard.
I can almost see Him...
Huge, Almighty, Father God...
bending over that board,
His chin in His hand,
as He carefully determines
the very best move for each of His children.

Texas

On the road again this morning. The Lord hasn't spoken to us about stopping at a campground or staying in any particular place thus far since we left Kingman, so we will continue to head east unless He shows us differently along the way.

Today, after John filled the motor home up with gas and got back behind the wheel, I said to him, "The next time we get gas, we'll probably need to use cash."

"Oh? Why?"

"Because the account is getting pretty low."

"Like how low?"

"Maybe $10."

He didn't say a word. Just looked at me and started the engine.

At this point, we were hundreds of miles from anyone we knew and anything we were familiar with. We did have some cash, but probably not enough to make it to Knoxville, Tennessee, to our daughter's house.

We didn't call anyone or even really cry out to God about it. When we stopped at another Walmart that night, during our time of prayer, we just told God that He had called us out here and He knew what our account looked like, so we were trusting Him to take care of us. And we went to sleep in peace.

The next morning a pastor's wife called us. She asked how we were doing and I told her we were fine.

Then she said, "I guess I should have asked how your account is doing."

That surprised me for her to ask about our account. I mumbled something like, "Oh, we have about $10 in there, but we're fine."

"$10!!!" she shouted. "You can't be out there doing the Lord's work on $10! Where can I go to deposit money?"

"Oh, you don't have to do that," I said.

"Oh, yes I do!" she said. "God woke me up this morning and told me I needed to put money in your account."

God sends angels in the natural
and angels in the supernatural
to do His bidding
and take care of His servants.
Thank You, Lord,
that You never forget us
and are always aware of our needs.

Louisiana

As we were traveling along, the Lord spoke clearly to me about stopping at a Cracker Barrel at the next exit. I told John I would go inside and look around to see what God had for us to do here. He could stretch out on the couch and rest for a little while.

Strolling through the store, I was on high alert. I knew God had sent me in here and didn't want to miss it. I didn't have to wait long.

A beautiful lady, who happened to be the manager, stopped to see if she could help me. I told her I was just looking around and then sensed I needed to say more.

"I am actually in here because God told my husband and I to stop at this Cracker Barrel," I said to her.

She grabbed my arm and almost pulled me over to the side so we could have a little corner to talk.

"Girl!" she said. "You are *kidding* me?"

Then after looking at me really good, she said, "You aren't kidding me."

"No ma'am, I'm very serious."

At that point, God gave me a word for her. He spoke to where she was at and to where He wanted her to go (spiritually). She wouldn't let go of me. She hugged and cried and hugged some more. Finally, she got herself together enough to speak. Then she told me she thought God had been speaking to her about some things, but she wasn't sure if it was God. She had really been struggling. Now she had her answer.

Unless I feel led to,
I don't usually share specifics
about a personal word for someone.

That word
is between them and God,
and not for the world to hear.

However, I don't believe this lady
will ever be the same.
All it takes is one word from God
to change our lives.

Once again, it's all about
obedience.

The Vision

I woke up at 12:30am the following morning from a dream. I knew I'd had a dream, but had absolutely no recollection of what it was about. As soon as I woke up, God began to speak this to me —

> **Draw near to God and He will draw near to you.**
> **If you do not draw near to God,**
> **you can expect His judgment to fall on you**
> **in a mighty way.**

I lay there for a few minutes trying to recall something about the dream. The Lord continued to speak those words over and over to me until I got up to write them down.

It was strange. The dream was completely gone, but the word remains so strong.

I had not intended
to write about this word
because I have nothing more
except the word itself.
No interpretation.
No dream.
No follow-up.
But God brought me
back to it again and again,

until I added it into the book.

This word is for someone
or many someones
who will read this.

Is it for you, dear one?

Unable to go back to bed right away, I read a few chapters in Acts. In chapters 16 and 17, I was reading about how Paul and Barnabas and all the disciples were led by the Holy Ghost. They didn't really have an agenda. If the Holy Spirit told them not to go somewhere, they simply turned aside and didn't go there.

I knew God was showing me how much this resembled John and I. Literally, this is our life. As I prayed, the Lord let me know that while these things seem strange to many, they wouldn't have seemed odd at all to those who were closest to Jesus.

Around 2:15am, I went back to bed. I just had to sing, so I lay in bed and sang a few hymns. John had been up, so he was still awake and started singing with me.

The Holy Spirit came over me and I began to speak in tongues.

Then I saw it!

This vision looked more like the Capitol building than the White House, but it seemed to be both. It looked like the dome of the Capitol building and then it kind of changed to the White House. It faded back and forth, back and forth, like one of those pictures that change as you move it.

I was still speaking in tongues but that, too, had changed. The tone was fierce and loud. So loud John actually said, "Shhh. Shhh." He never says anything, but this was our first night in a campground in days and he may have thought I would disturb the people next door. I heard him, but could no more speak softer than I could stop speaking.

Then my right arm bent at the elbow with my hand straight up and began to fall to the right side. This happened over and over again. I cannot begin to say how many times. And these words came out of my mouth over and over

"The White House is divided and it cannot stand!"
"The White House is divided and it cannot stand!"
"The White House is divided and it cannot stand!"

It was a loud, fierce voice that did not sound like my own.

Then I saw the crack. It was huge and it looked like a perfectly straight line from top to bottom. It began just at the right edge of the top of the dome and came straight down, almost but not quite, in the middle. And once again the White House appeared to be transposed over the Capitol building. And then it broke. The right side just fell over.

And I was quiet and still.

> *I have experienced many things*
> *in the Spirit,*
> *but never anything quite like that.*
> *It was very powerful!*
> *The force I felt as those words*
> *came out of my mouth*
> *cannot even be described.*
> *There is often just no way to*
> *truly describe*
> *the supernatural moving*
> *of God.*

Getting back up out of bed, (there was no way I could just go to sleep after that) I asked, "What do you want me to do with this, Lord?"

Immediately, a passage in Ephesians came to me.

[10]FINALLY, MY BRETHREN, BE STRONG IN THE LORD, AND IN THE POWER OF HIS MIGHT.
[11]PUT ON THE WHOLE ARMOUR OF GOD,

THAT YE MAY BE ABLE TO STAND
AGAINST THE WILES OF THE DEVIL.
[12]FOR WE WRESTLE NOT AGAINST FLESH AND BLOOD,
BUT AGAINST PRINCIPALITIES,
AGAINST POWERS,
AGAINST THE RULERS OF THE DARKNESS
OF THIS WORLD,
AGAINST SPIRITUAL WICKEDNESS IN HIGH PLACES.
[13]WHEREFORE TAKE UNTO YOU THE WHOLE ARMOUR
OF GOD, THAT YOU MAY BE ABLE TO WITHSTAND
IN THE EVIL DAY,
AND HAVING DONE ALL, TO STAND.

EPHESIANS 6:10-13 (KJV)

I believe God gave this to me as a word for His people. Regardless of what we see or hear, no matter what is taking place in our nation, this word is for all of us.

Be strong in the Lord...

After praying a while longer, I was almost ready to go back to bed when I heard it. A howl. Three or Four times. At first, I thought it was just an animal outside somewhere, then I realized my dog was acting really strange. Had it been another animal out there, he would have been barking. Instead, he was growling, low and fierce. He kept on for a few minutes.

Then I began to feel the evil. It permeated the air briefly and I could almost smell it. I knew it wasn't just an animal out there. Whatever was there had been sent by the enemy.

And I knew what to do! I commanded it to leave in the name of Jesus.

It wasn't long before my dog stopped growling and the sense of evil I had was gone.

Thank You, Lord,
that You have made a way for us.
You did not leave us helpless
and weak.

146

You did not leave us without
provision
for all situations.
We need only to trust You,
stand strong,
and say,
"In the name of Jesus."

Trust in the Lord with all your heart
and do not lean
on your own understanding.
In all your ways acknowledge Him,
and He will make your paths straight.

Proverbs 3:5-6 (NASB)

January 2013

On January 11th, 2013, God gave John and I another blessing. Our son and daughter-in-law had a baby girl. Her name is Messer Lyric and we thank God for her. We now have eight grandchildren, four boys and four girls. Welcome to our family, Baby Messer! What a great way to bring in the New Year!

In early January I had some meetings scheduled in Columbia, South Carolina. The night before we were to leave, I asked the Lord if He had a message for the people I would be speaking to. At 6:47am on January 7th, the Lord gave this word to me.

> I have heard their cry.
> I am giving them more time before
> the storm.
>
> The storm will still come,
> but I am delaying things to give them
> more time to prepare.
>
> Many in this area have been faithful
> to pray sacrificially and repent.
> I will honor that.
>
> The storm will not be as fierce,
> the judgment will not be as
> devastating in this area because of it.

God continued to open doors for meetings during our time in this area. We had intended to be here for five days; we ended up staying for five weeks. More and more people were asking us to come.

An opportunity to speak at a large church in Columbia was a huge blessing to John and I. It was wonderful to get these words from the Lord out to so many people in just two services.

As I was preparing to speak at that church, the Lord said to me —

My child, I will speak to you now.
Listen and write.

Many children will suffer because
their parents wouldn't listen.

Wives will suffer because their
husbands wouldn't listen.

Just as the Israelites didn't like
the change in their lives when
they were brought out of Egypt,
and so they rebelled,
the same will happen here in America.

Many will not listen.
Many will rebel.

But I still have a remnant.
It is small, but growing.

And they are listening.
They are not going to rebel
when times get tough
and their comforts are taken away.

They are going to move with Me.
They are going to stay under My shelter.
And they will be My harvesters
when the time is ready.

God had been giving me Joshua chapter 1 since shortly after the first of the year. Considering the number of times God led me to this portion of scripture, I knew He wanted me to really get hold of it. It wasn't enough to just read it or even remember it, but I believe God wants His people to hide this in their hearts and it will help to carry us through.

BE STRONG AND COURAGEOUS. (VS. 6)

BE STRONG AND VERY COURAGEOUS. TURN NOT TO THE RIGHT HAND NOR THE LEFT FROM FOLLOWING MY WORD. (VS. 7)

HAVE I NOT COMMANDED YOU? BE STRONG, BE COURAGEOUS, BE NOT AFRAID NOR DISMAYED. FOR THE LORD THY GOD IS WITH YOU WHEREVER YOU GO. (VS. 9)

...ONLY BE STRONG AND OF GOOD COURAGE. (VS. 18)

*These are only a few nuggets
that especially stood out to me.
I would encourage you all
to read the entire chapter of Joshua 1.
Not just once, but often.
Let it sink into your spirit.
Be strong and courageous,
for the Lord your God is with you
wherever you go.*

But from there
you will seek the Lord your God,
and you will find Him
if you search for Him
with all your heart and all your soul.

Deuteronomy 4:29 (NASB)

Shaking Off the Dust

This was turning into a year where we could hardly keep up with the calls that were coming in asking if I would come and speak. In March we went back to Chicago. I spoke on a Saturday afternoon to a group of about forty people. They were mostly ladies, but a few men. One of the men came in with his arms crossed over his chest and sat that way almost the entire meeting. Everyone else seemed open to hear what the Lord was saying.

At one point, God just veered me off the path of what I was speaking about and took me to Colossians 3. I told them God was speaking to me about unforgiveness and someone there, possibly more than one, had unforgiveness in their heart. Many of the people in attendance responded to that, including the man with his arms across his chest. It was amazing what God did in the middle of that meeting.

We got back on course and continued. God gave me a word for this group about standing. I knew it was for others as well.

Stand. You must learn to stand.

**There will be much persecution,
especially in this area.**

If you have prepared in your heart

**ahead of time, it will be much
easier to take a firm stand for Christ
when the time comes.**

Are you ready to stand?

Near the end of the meeting, God prompted me to give the word about Facebook. I was a little hesitant. The meeting had been good, really good, and I was concerned people might be put off with that Facebook word.

But God continued to let me know I must give it, so I did. The response was amazing. There were so many who were in agreement, including two ladies who were involved in ministry at the church. They came to me after the meeting in tears. One of them had been concerned for quite some time because all the information for the youth activities goes out over Facebook. This means the teenagers have to be on Facebook if they want to know what's going on for them at church. We talked and prayed about the situation. Most people stayed for a while when the meeting was over, even though it had lasted about three hours.

There was one more meeting scheduled for Monday evening. If it was anything like this, that would be a huge blessing. We had seen God move in mighty power today.

However, the Monday night meeting was not to be. An email came in to my friend who had set the meetings up. It wasn't a very kind email where I was concerned, and accused me of things that simply weren't true. And to top it all off, this email had gone out to an entire group of ladies.

I knew before we even read all the way to the bottom what it was really about. By the time we got to the end it was confirmed. The real problem was the word about social media that didn't sit well with some of the staff. They had canceled the meeting for Monday night.

I had never been treated in such a way, and was truly distraught about it. I left a voicemail for one of the pastors, asking if we could meet before my husband and I had to leave the area, to straighten out the problem. He didn't return my call.

There were ladies who called to offer their home for the meeting, but I didn't feel that would be the right thing to do considering the situation. I told them possibly God would bring me back at some point and then meetings could be scheduled at other places.

John and I left a few days later. God had brought peace about the situation, but it still bothered me.

We need to talk about this Facebook word for a moment. You know, I have been giving people words from the Lord for almost twenty years and I have never, ever had the response I have gotten from this word. That, in itself, should tell us something. When people, from all walks of life, will receive all kinds of words from the Lord, and then a word having to do with social media brings such a firestorm, that should tell us where peoples' priorities lie.

It isn't like I beat them over the head with that word, or threaten them if they don't delete their account. I simply give the word that was given to me by God. They are free to do what they wish with that word. And as I always tell people before a meeting (and sometimes after), take everything I tell you back to the Lord. Pray about it, and see what He would have you to do with each and every thing. Ask God how this applies to you and, if you don't know, put that word on the shelf and wait to hear from the Lord about it.

Somehow people are able to do that with most any word – except one about getting off Facebook! Never have I heard so many excuses about something. The top two amaze me. The two reasons most Christians say they can't get off Facebook are, one - because that's how they keep up with their kids and see pictures of their grandchildren; two - they use it for ministry. I am not disputing that those sound like good reasons to stay on there, but did we have a life before Facebook? How did we see pictures of grandchildren and minister to people just a few years ago? I have had people say horrible things about me, stop speaking to me, and even put out terrible things over social media about me. All because of this word. If we as Christians are this addicted to Facebook, we had better get on our faces before God.

> *I cannot say God didn't warn me.*
> *He did, very clearly,*
> *and I still don't like to give that word.*
> *But I try to be obedient*
> *each and every time*
> *He prompts me to give it,*
> *regardless of the cost.*
>
> *I ask each of you*
> *to go to the back of the book*
> *where the words from the Lord*
> *are listed,*
> *and read this word again.*
> *Then sincerely pray about it.*
> *If it doesn't apply to you,*
> *disregard it.*
> *But don't ever say*
> *you weren't warned,*
> *because the alarm*
> *has been sounded.*

A God Appointment

In April, 2013, we had to pull over to the side of the road. There was smoke coming from somewhere. We couldn't even tell where it was coming from. After calling roadside assistance, we made some coffee and sat down to wait. There wasn't much room on the shoulder and, every time a big truck went by, the motor home would rock. It seemed those trucks were just inches from us. But the peace of God is amazing! There we sat, smiling at each other, waiting for the mechanic to show up.

It was about 45 minutes later when the two young men arrived. They located the problem quickly. It was a broken hose and they just happened to have the right one with them. The only charge to us was $30 and they were apologetic for that. They seemed surprised at how nice we were to them. I suppose most people who are stranded by the side of the road are so frustrated that they aren't very pleasant to the mechanics who come to help them, especially if they've waited a long while.

God had spoken to me, while they were putting on the new hose, that we should give them Bibles. We had been chatting with them about what we were doing and about the Lord. Before they left, we asked if we could pray for them and if they would like a Bible. Both young men responded warmly and one had tears in his eyes after we prayed a short prayer for them. We gave them each a nice Bible and they went on their way. We noticed they carried their Bibles almost reverently. John and I both agreed our breakdown had been a God appointment for those young men.

A Prophet or A King

In early April the Lord began to speak to me about the mess our country is in. I would pray and ask Him questions and He gave me answers. Possibly not the answers I wanted to hear, but I knew it was truth.

I was reading in 1 Samuel 8, where Samuel was old and had made his sons judges over Israel. His sons weren't Godly men, as their father had been. And seeing their sinfulness and pride, Israel decided they no longer wanted to be led by a prophet or judge. They wanted a king like all the other nations. Samuel wasn't pleased by this, but God told him to give them a king if that was what they wanted.

Israel thought their problems were from a faulty government, when in reality every issue they faced could be traced to their own sin, and specifically, their rejection of God's leadership over their nation.

Today, many Godly men and women want to blame the government for the problems in our nation. No. Our government is not what it should be, but it is our sin, as the Church, that has driven this country into its current chaos.

We have voted these people into high ranking political positions, and then sat back and watched while they perverted the offices they sat in. Power and money do terrible things to people. It takes a very strong man or woman of God to stand for what is right when power and money are on the line.

Our country has been off track for a long, long time. And as with any wrong path we get on, the farther we go, the harder it is to get back.

We cannot sit back and blame the government. It all begins with us. The Church should have been taking a stand years ago. We had freedoms we should have been exercising. Where has the Church been while those freedoms are being taken away from us?

I can tell you where the Church has been. We have been sitting behind stained glass windows, or building new, fancy buildings. Sitting in church, listening to another "feel good" sermon. We have been planning another program, so they will come.

And if we are going to take a stand to claim our country for God, we're going to have to get outside the church building to do it!

Pastors are going to have to stop worrying about numbers and start concentrating on hearts, beginning with their own. If this country is going to turn back to God, if we are to have an awakening, it must begin with each individual heart. We must repent and turn back to God as individuals before we can hope to change a nation.

Alabama and Georgia

A pastor had asked us to come to Dauphin Island, Alabama. God had shown us the time was to be now, so in April of 2013 we made our first trip to the island. John and I had no idea how God would use us here, nor of the strong bond that would develop. Not only between us and the church we worked with while we were here, but with the people of the island, as well.

God gave me a dream the first night we were on the island. The campground we stayed in was directly across the road from where the ferry came in.

In this dream, I was standing near where the ferry would normally be, but a huge ship was there instead. It was massive! Very tall, so much so that I felt just inches tall standing in front of it.

The next thing I knew, I had been lifted up to stand on the bow of the ship. As I looked down inside, I saw it was completely full of people. There was standing room only.

They all seemed to be wearing tattered looking shifts, faded light blue in color. All of their heads were shaved. I noticed a little hair had grown back out on some people, so it appeared their heads hadn't all been shaved at the same time. The hair that was growing back in looked to be white. I was unable to tell the women from the men. Most were adults, but there were some children.

Someone looked up and saw me and they all began to reach up to me and call out for help. When they tipped their faces up toward me, I could see their cheeks were sunken in. Then I noticed how thin they were and wondered if they were starving.

I didn't see anyone (like guards or soldiers) keeping them on the ship. I wondered why they didn't just get off. Quite possibly, the guards were there and I just couldn't see them though.

Twenty-four hours later, the Lord gave me a word for the pastor here.

> **Many, many will come here**
> **starving for the word of God.**
> **Hundreds, even.**
>
> **They must be discipled!**
>
> **Stop all foolishness!**
> **And get down to business!**
>
> **Your people must be discipled**
> **so they can disciple others.**
>
> **Your army must be ready**
> **to fight for the Living God!**

Trials and Smiles

A couple of days later, we had severe thunderstorms with a lot of wind. John noticed water dripping from a spot in the ceiling. Soon, it was pouring in. Had we not been home it would have been a disaster, but we were able to catch most of the water in pans and garbage cans, and soak the rest up with towels.

God began to speak to us about not giving up. He continued to encourage us as we got things cleaned up and dried out.

In the middle of all this, John had gotten a lot of bites on his legs. We weren't familiar with no-see-ums (yes, there really is an insect with that name), but we got more familiar with them than we ever wanted to.

We were only on the island one week, but by the time we left, John had over 200 bites on his lower legs. As he drove through Florida, heading north into Georgia for our next series of meetings, I knew we were going to have to get some medical attention for him. I had anointed and prayed for him, but he was still getting worse. I thought he must be having an allergic reaction to the bites because I could see hives popping out on his arms as he drove. I asked God to get us to the hospital where John could get the care he needed.

The man who had invited us to come to South Georgia met us outside town and, after we parked the motor home, he took us to the emergency room. The staff took excellent care of John, recognizing immediately that he was in trouble and needed care. After IVs, a shot, and prescriptions, we were on our way. It took two full days for John to get back to normal, but we were very thankful for the great care he had received.

There are those who ask me,
"Why does God sometimes just heal
and other times we have to get
medical attention?"
I do not have an answer
for that question.
All I can say is that
God is sovereign
and we must trust Him
regardless.
We aren't always going
to understand the whys,
but we can always know
He does all things for the good
of those who love Him.

The meetings in Georgia were good. Three distinct differences stood out to me there, more than in most other places.

There were those who were totally on board, who understood and received the message from the Lord.

Then there were those who were just indifferent. They didn't seem to care one way or the other.

And then there were those who wanted to argue about the Facebook word. I don't argue with anyone about any word from the Lord. I may discuss it briefly, but people need to take those things back to God. I'm just the messenger.

I was encouraged by two teenage girls who agreed with the word about Facebook and were confident enough to stand up and make a statement. They had both been on Facebook long enough to see the damage it was doing and were both going home to delete their accounts.

It amazes me how the younger generation
often seems to have a better grasp
of radical things of the Lord.

My generation wants things
in a nice little box
all tied up with a bow.
Oh, and plenty of tape on the box,
so nothing can get out.

Not everyone, of course,
but many are like this.
If it doesn't fit in their box,
They don't want any part of it.
It takes them out of their comfort zone.

We need to be hungry
for the things of God.
We need to be open
to the moving of the Holy Spirit.
And we need to understand that

Jesus never put things in a box,
nor was He willing to be put into one.

Speaking of the younger generation, I am reminded of a young man who started teaching at a Christian school. It was a Lutheran School.

I had met him at a small group one evening, and the Holy Spirit kept reminding me all evening that I needed to go out to the car to get a copy of my book, *From Our Wicked Ways*, to give him.

At the end of the meeting, I gave him a copy of the book, not expecting to hear any more about it.

Just this spring, I saw him again. He told me that book had changed his life and the lives of his 22 students! He went into a bit of detail, which I won't share here, but he read that book out loud to his students. Not many teachers would have been bold enough to do that. This young teacher stepped out and gave his students more than just religion in a box. He gave them gold nuggets they could apply to everyday life, things they could relate to. He taught them who they were in Christ, and lives were changed.

Chicago Revisited

It had been three months since the incident in Chicago where the meeting had been canceled. I was surprised when the Lord began to speak to me about going back there. I hadn't expected to go back for a year or even longer. Obviously God had other plans.

Normally, when we go to Illinois, we don't take the motor home because there are people we can stay with when we get there. This time, God was saying we needed to take the motor home and stay for at least a month. I knew He had a lot of things for us to do if we were to stay that long.

The campgrounds in that area are full during the summer months. The residents take their campers and leave them there all summer so they can go out on weekends or for a week at a time. I had contacted a campground that would be centrally located for us and she offered to put us on a waiting list in case something opened up. That was in early May.

Later on in May, I began to get emails and phone calls from people who wanted to host a meeting in Chicago. I knew God was giving us the "go ahead" to continue with our plans. He would take care of the details.

We felt that mid-June was the time we should head to Illinois, so we continued to make plans to go. Those who knew of our plans were getting concerned when, by June, we still didn't have any options available for camping once we arrived. John and I weren't troubled by this. We knew we had heard God and we were simply following orders.

The day before we were to leave for Illinois I received a call from the campground. A spot had just opened up and would be available for six to eight weeks if we wanted it. I told her we would take it for four weeks. We had walked by faith, and not by sight, as we continued to prepare to go to Illinois; God had provided.

Unto the Hills

I woke up early on Tuesday, June 11th. I glanced out the windows of the motor home in the early morning light. The words of Psalm 121 began to come to me.

> [1]I WILL LIFT UP MY EYES UNTO THE HILLS,
> FROM WHENCE COMETH MY HELP.
> [2]MY HELP COMES FROM THE LORD,
> WHICH MADE HEAVEN AND EARTH.
> [3]HE WILL NOT SUFFER THY FOOT TO BE MOVED:
> HE THAT KEEPETH THEE WILL NOT SLUMBER.
> [4]BEHOLD, HE THAT KEEPETH ISRAEL
> SHALL NEITHER SLUMBER NOR SLEEP.
> [5]THE LORD IS THEY KEEPER:
> THE LORD IS THY SHADE UPON THY RIGHT HAND.
> [6]THE SUN SHALL NOT SMITE THEE BY DAY,
> NOR THE MOON BY NIGHT.
> [7]THE LORD SHALL PRESERVE THEE FROM ALL EVIL:
> HE SHALL PRESERVE THY SOUL.
> [8]THE LORD SHALL PRESERVE THY GOING OUT
> AND THY COMING IN FROM THIS TIME FORTH,
> AND EVEN FOR EVERMORE.
> PSALM 121 (KJV)

I know this Psalm well, but I don't quote it often. It just seemed to burst forth from my heart this morning. Lord, what do You want to tell me about this? Immediately He answered.

Remember where your help comes from.

**In the near future, remember this
strongly.**

**You need to know this.
Know this well.
You won't be able to rely
on anyone else
Just remember it.
You will soon understand it better.**

*This sounded rather ominous.
I think I liked it better
before I asked the Lord
what He wanted to tell me
about that psalm this morning.
I liked looking out at the morning haze
over the hills and trees
and having that psalm
burst forth like a song.*

*But obviously I needed to hear
what the Lord was telling me.
I didn't understand why,
but it was best that I didn't know.*

Within the next three days, we had leaking transmission seals that had to be repaired. While the motor home was in the shop, a lady hit our car while it was parked and we almost couldn't drive it, and our daughter called to say our little granddaughter had put her hand on a grill and was being transferred to another hospital by ambulance from the ER.

I sent out a call to our prayer warriors. One of them sent a text back simply saying "Psalm 121." Yes! We had to remember our help comes from the Lord. If He made the heavens and the earth, He can certainly take care of us.

At the repair shop, they had pulled a truck out of one of the bays in order to get us back on the road and probably didn't charge us half of what it should have been. The lady's insurance would take care of our car. We would have it repaired once we got to Illinois.

Most importantly, Juliet's hand was going to be okay. Praise Jesus for always taking care of us!

Just a couple of days later, we arrived safely at our campground in central Illinois.

A Word Appears

It was Sunday night around 11pm on June 16th. I had felt a need to work on this book, so I got out my laptop and sat down to write. As I pulled up a blank document, another document popped up on my screen. It was in a totally different font and program from anything else on my laptop. I would have deleted it, except that I recognized it as something the Lord had spoken to me years before. I didn't know how many years, but I knew it had been a long time.

> My people are going about in their
> usual manner.
> The Church is still interested in
> meetings and programs.
> If ever there was a time for
> sackcloth and ashes, it is now.
>
> Your country is in deep trouble,
> My child.
> Many people recognize it,
> believers and unbelievers alike.
> The difference is, the believers
> should know what to do about it,
> but there are very few on their
> faces to Me.
>
> Now is the time for crying out to God,
> for fasting, for sacrifice.
> Judgment is at hand!
>
> If you could see ahead,
> you would shake with fear.

But there is no need to fear.
I will take care of My own.

I will hide them under My wings
until the calamity has passed.
But they need to be in prayer,
repenting, fasting, crying out
for mercy and for the
judgment to be lessened.

The time is now!
Don't wait until it is too late!

This word from the Lord was actually on the laptop that I had before this one. I have no idea how it got on my newer computer. It took a little while, but I finally tracked it down. God originally gave this word to me October 26th, 2008 at 3:16am.

It was written in my journal from that time, and I located it on my old laptop. I had completely forgotten about it. It has been almost five years since the Lord gave this to me. He obviously wanted to bring it to my attention at this time.

Ears to Hear

The last week of June I went to the Chicago area to stay with my friend, Cindy. John took me to meet her and then drove back to stay in the motor home at the campground.

Cindy had organized some meetings and, after I arrived, more people asked me to speak. I ended up speaking at seven meetings in five days. Some of those meetings lasted four to five hours. Most of them were ladies' groups, and they just didn't seem to want to leave. We all had a great time hearing from the Lord and watching Him touch those who had asked for prayer.

During one of those meetings, a sweet lady by the name of Nikki gave us a testimony about how God got her off Facebook.

I asked her if she would email her testimony to me. Here it is, in Nikki's words.

My Facebook Testimony
By Nikki

A couple years ago, I had the privilege of meeting Maxie and hearing her share her testimony about what the Lord was doing in their lives. That first time, I was deeply moved by the Spirit to the point of tears. It frankly took me by surprise how I reacted to her and her husband's story of obedience. I could see parallels in my life and I felt the Spirit opening my heart with longing for that kind of posture to listen and obey.

After that time, I would get updates on their travels through a mutual friend and one particular occasion, I believe in the late summer, she sent out a link to a message Maxie had given to a congregation in their travels. I remember listening with headphones on, in my bed one night. I honestly don't remember anything about the message (I assume it was her word to the pastors about repenting) because at some point she spoke about the dangers of Facebook, that it had become an idol to people and that in the future it would be used to persecute the church.
At the instant she said the word Facebook, my pulse quickened and I felt flushed; an immediate visceral reaction to her words.

I remember saying, "Lord, what's that about?" But in my Spirit I knew there was truth in Maxie's words.

You see, with encouragement/exhortation being one of my natural given gifts, Facebook was one of my means of keeping connected with friends and family. I'm not one to talk on the phone a lot, so FB allowed me to speak (or write) words of life, comment on pictures, give an uplifting phrase to those who needed it. I even looked at it a bit like an extension of my ministry, touching others with the love of Jesus. BUT, I would find myself in the spare minutes of my day, scrolling through the feed to see what was going on and who needed some love. Spare minutes I could never get back... spare minutes better spent on REAL LIFE, not cyber life.

When I heard Maxie's words, I felt deep conviction about the AMOUNT of time I was spending there and asked God to help me commit to consciously cut back, catch myself when my hands went to grab my phone and mindlessly scroll. There is only room for one God on the Throne and you know those idols, they like to creep up there and take their place with Him. Honestly, I truly believe He enabled me to do this and I felt that it was a right response to the conviction I felt when I heard the message.

The fall and winter months pass and I continued my measured use of Facebook. Quite frankly, I found the pull to go online lessening through this season. I was amazed when days would go by without me checking on Facebook at all. I give all glory to God for the way He tempered my habit with self-control, slowly taking away the urge to check when I had a free moment. He gave me the gift of being fully present instead.

So, on a Saturday in March, Maxie came to our church again and God made a way for me to join the group. She updated us on what the Lord has been up to in their lives and gave a good word exhorting us to "Stand, stand! You must learn to stand for ME!" says the Lord. She finished, opened the discussion up to questions and one woman asked about her message regarding Facebook. Immediately the Spirit in me caused a physical reaction, almost a fight or flight warning and to be honest, it was a little freaky.

"Why, Lord?"

She gave her warning again that all believers need to get off Facebook, this time even speaking about people using it as a platform to spread the Gospel. Even with this seemingly good use of the media outlet, she still felt the word she got from the Lord stands firm.

With the response of the Spirit in me, I definitely took notice. I wondered why I was still reacting this way when He had done such a work in me over the months. I could honestly say Facebook was not an idol in my life the way it had been in seasons past.

"Hadn't I been obedient, Lord?"

I came home and journaled that night. The following is my entry, the Lord speaking to me.

Saturday, March 16th, 2013

> "I am always speaking to you, dear child.
> Are you listening?
> Distractions close your eyes and ears to Me.
> You know my voice.
> Repent, forgive, prepare for the harvest.
> I am always for you, my child.
> I will tell you. Get up with Me.
> I am working on your heart,
> preparing you for even greater love.
> Stand for Me. In Me! Get in the Word.
> Get more of the Word."

What does it look like for me to STAND UP for YOU?

> "DO NOT let your eyes move from Me.
> Listen for me and obey when I ask of you.
> Do not move until I tell you.
> Keep asking until you hear.
> My eagles will carry you to safety. (Exodus 19:4)"

The next morning (Sunday), I awoke excited to go worship with my church family. Our family arrived, I get the children to their respective classes and head into service with praise music already playing. It dawns on me there that I cannot hear well out of my right ear. Someone tries to talk to me in that ear and I have to redirect her to the other ear. I try to pull on it, to pop it, but nothing changed. So strange. And for the record, I cannot remember EVER having an ear infection! I am prone to having swollen tonsils when I get sick but never any issues with my ears. I figured I must have some fluid that is causing this but it seems strange because I am not sick in the least, no stuffy, runny nose, no pain or any issues at all, just CAN'T HEAR!

I don't think too much about it at the time, just a bit annoying and I assume it will get better as I am active throughout the day.

I journaled with God that day and don't even mention it. He says to me:

> "You have wasted too much time.
> Media is your idol.
> I know your love for me
> but the time has come for
> wholehearted study in My Word."

Wow. Forceful words for a person who thought she was managing that part of her life quite well. Ok, Lord.

Monday — My hearing is still gone and I have NO pain, but at times it feels like I'm drowning, very claustrophobic for some reason and causes a panic to come over me. I'm not prone to anxiety, so this is a strange and unnerving feeling. I even go to our chiropractor who says I should get relief and my hearing back by the afternoon.

I laughingly say, "Unless the Lord says otherwise!" and believe it is so.

Monday night comes with no change but much clarity. My journal entry:

This is day two of You closing my right ear to hearing about 40%. I think it is beautiful and appropriate, as I needed the extra encouragement after Maxie spoke about getting off Facebook – almost like Jonah in the whale can only think of how to obey now that You've got his attention.

I don't want to be hard hearted to You! Do whatever it takes to help me listen, sweet Lord!

> "You heard me correctly.
> The time is short, child!
> We must get to work.

I will soften your heart to reach out
to those I prompt you to.
I AM working.
I know you want my heart.
I am giving it to you.
To be broken over what I care about.
I am drawing your babies to Me.
Stand! Be my warrior!
The battle is already at hand."

It is clear. He wants me to deactivate my Facebook account.

Tuesday morning comes with no change in my hearing.

I grab my phone and ask the Lord to help me write a post for all of my FB friends explaining why I will be leaving the fold. It takes awhile and I'm surprised at how long it took me to press the POST button. I knew the Lord was calling me to this, but it was still hard.

Was I silly to connect my hearing loss to leaving Facebook? Does He do things like this? I'm sure there's a medical reason for this, just go to the doctor... all these things rushing through my head telling me not to do it.

I finally press POST. Immediately I start getting responses of encouragement, "I'll miss you," and other messages of astonishment and love. I let it sit in cyberspace a few hours so more people can see before I finally sign off. I have to say it was bittersweet. How would I see pictures of the babies far away? I did have feelings of loss and sadness as I realized I would lose the easy connection I had to all these precious people. BUT, my resolve still remained.

I even thought, "What if you don't get your hearing back even after you sign off?" Oh well, at least I was obedient to what I THOUGHT God was telling me. His ways are higher than mine and He knows my heart.

The morning passed with messages coming in. And around noon I began to sense something happening with my ear. A minute change, something was happening.

A couple more hours with my ear slowly continuing to get better, I read the final comments, posted a few more replies.

At about 2:30pm I officially deactivated my account. By 3pm my hearing was back to 100%. I was PRAISING the LORD and doing a happy dance.

I later journaled:

Obedience brings blessing! That evening I started to have some pain in my ear and a sore throat so an ear infection was likely the culprit, but love that you use it (cause it) to bring me close to you! Beautiful!

And I love that He allowed me no pain or sore throat when I was going through it so I couldn't explain it away as just me being sick!

This past year without Facebook has been such a growth year for me, undoubtedly richer without the distraction of this media outlet. It was odd at first and I missed catching up with people, but God was gracious through it all.

There are always things that want to climb up on the altar to replace the ones dethroned, so just being attentive to His voice about all of it has kept me following and listening, ready to obey His call. Thankful beyond measure!

WOW! What an amazing testimony! There is nothing I could add to that to make it any more powerful. Thank You, Nikki.

I could fill an entire book
(or at least a few chapters)
if I wrote about all the miracles
and awesome things that took place
in those meetings.
But we'll leave that for another time.

I was soon to understand
why the Lord had
given me Psalm 121.
My faith would be taken
to a new level.

Trust and Obey

Cindy had planned to drive me back to central Illinois on Monday and stay with John and I a few days, but I had a strong sense I needed to go back on Sunday. We arrived Sunday afternoon. I was exhausted from all the meetings and rested when we got there. But by Monday morning, I was ready to get going again, and Cindy and I took a bike ride around the campground. When we were almost back to our campsite, I saw John walking toward us. I could tell something was wrong. He told me he had terrible chest pain and needed to go to the hospital. Cindy offered to stay there with our dog so we wouldn't need to be concerned about anything, and I drove John to the emergency room.

Although I was concerned, I really thought they would find the problem and within a few hours we would be heading back.

Boy, was I wrong. They did find the problem in a few hours, but John was not going home with me. They admitted him. He had severe pneumonia and they found a mass on his right lung the size of an orange!

Later that night, after he was settled into his room, I drove back to the campground. I had called the kids to let them know and others that I knew would be praying. Having lived there most of my life, I had family and a lot of friends within a few miles of the campground. They all said they would be praying and most of them wanted to know what I was going to do.

"I'm going to trust God," was my constant answer.

For the first two days, John was really sick. He had to be on oxygen and could hardly get enough air in his lungs to talk. The nurses and aides would come in and talk to us. John had managed to talk to them enough to tell them we were traveling across the country calling America back to God.

It seemed one nurse would leave and another nurse or aide would come in. I believe every one of them could sense the presence of the Lord in that room, even if some of them didn't realize what it was. Most of them asked us questions, and quite a few had troubles they needed to share. We knew the staff was drawn to us because they needed something from God. And of course, God didn't let them down. He gave us the words they needed to hear. John and I were both so blessed to be able to minister to them.

John spent five days in the hospital. I believe it was the third day when he had another scan to check the mass. One of his doctors came in later and John asked him if the mass was really the size of an orange. The doctor said he would go back and look at the chart to make sure. He came back shortly to say it was very small, the size of a pea. Needless to say, we were thrilled! God was definitely at work!

Cindy left to go back to Chicago, and the nights were long. I did a lot of praying. I cried out to God asking Him why this couldn't have happened someplace where we would have had a line of pastors coming in to anoint him and pray. Or why we couldn't at least have been close to one of the kids when it happened, so I wouldn't feel so alone. He didn't give me answers to all of my questions, He just told me to trust Him.

While thinking about
all that had
happened to us
in the past few weeks,
I was reminded of a note
I had written in my journal
a couple of months earlier,

while listening to a pastor
in Columbia, South Carolina.

You're not where you are because
the Lord is displeased
with you.
You are in this battle because
the devil knows
the Lord is pleased with you
and he is trying to take you out
or at least
immobilize you.

The doctors were saying John would need to make an appointment for a biopsy, and possibly surgery, after he was released from the hospital. They gave us the numbers and I called to make the appointments, but didn't truly feel we would stay in Illinois to do all that.

Finally, John was better and was able to come home. I lay awake that first night, so thankful he was beside me, and yet wondering about what would lie ahead. We both wanted to head south, but I knew John wasn't strong enough yet to drive the motor home that far and to hook up the car dolly. I could drive if I had to, but I wasn't strong enough to even budge that dolly.

And people continued to ask what we were going to do...and I continued to give them the same answer. We would trust God.

On July 11th, I woke up in the night to hear the Lord say to me —

Stay put until this is over.

God knew exactly when I needed to hear that, but it was not what I wanted to hear. I didn't want to stay put. John was getting his strength back and we both wanted to leave. This wasn't a horrible place. Not at all. Our family and friends had rallied around us and they were great. But we wanted to go home. We always said wherever we were was home but, in this crisis, we wanted to go south. That felt more like home to us.

I argued with God about this. I told Him they have doctors and they can do tests and biopsies in the south, too. We didn't *have* to be here. But God didn't change His mind and He made sure I was reminded of it. Every few days He would say in that still, small voice —

> **Stay put until it's over.**
> **My child, stay put until it's over.**

When He would tell me this in the middle of the night, I would be at peace. However, by the next day, I would try to tell myself that maybe I wasn't really hearing God. I didn't even realize at the time exactly what I was doing.

And then the next day He said to me —

> **Stay put until it's over, My child.**
> **Stay put until it's over.**
> **It will be over and then you**
> **can move on.**
> **Just stay put until it's over.**

His voice was so gentle. He knew what we were going through even better than we knew ourselves.

God had been clear about the church we should attend that Sunday. We heard a very interesting message about false prophets. It was taken from Jeremiah 23.

He spoke about how false prophets give you false hope. They say what the people *want* to hear, not what they *need* to hear. They say, "Peace, peace, when there is no peace."

False prophets do not speak truth and are not sent by God. Throughout all time, people have been persecuted for speaking truth. The world will love you if you tell them what they want to hear, but just because it's what people want to hear, doesn't mean it will benefit them.

He also used Micah 2:11, where it says if the people heard a prophecy of prosperity and plenty of wine, they would welcome that prophet.

It was an interesting message. He had a lot of good points, and God used that message to remind me that I still had a job to do. Even though some didn't welcome the message God had given me, many were waiting with open hearts and outstretched arms, just waiting for us to come.

The pastor invited us to lunch, and John and I were invited to come to a small group meeting later in the week by a couple from that church. It was great to have a sense of belonging. We sure missed the fellowship of our church.

And God was at it again. Monday morning at 2am I was awake just talking to Him when He told me —

Sit still until it's over.

He knows our thoughts
even before we are aware
of them ourselves.
He knew,
somewhere deep inside,
I was still yearning to leave.
And He wasn't going
to let me make that mistake.
He knew I would be obedient
with a few reminders
now and then.

We should be so thankful
He doesn't give up on us.

John and I went to the small group meeting. We didn't realize until we arrived that they wanted me to speak to the group. It was fine. I always feel prepared, even at a moments notice. I know that is from God. I certainly couldn't do that on my own! It was really a pretty large group and they were great people. We enjoyed being with them.

When I finished speaking they had some questions.

One man asked me, "What do you call yourself?"

I told him I call myself a watchman. A watchman on the wall. (I'm not always comfortable when people call me a prophet, as they often do.)

That night the Lord spoke to me about this.

> My daughter, listen to Me!
> Hold your head high, My daughter.
> Do not be ashamed of
> your calling as a prophet.
> I – and I only – have put you there.
> And only I can take you down.
> Never be embarrassed of what
> I have given you.
> I love you, My child,
> and I will only give you
> good things.

I sure had some repenting to do. I had indeed felt uncomfortable when that man asked me what I called myself. Even though he didn't say it, I knew he was wondering if I was a prophet. I should have just told him that God has called me to be a prophet. If I have another opportunity to speak to that man, I will do just that.

The day finally came for John's biopsy. We were both feeling a little anxious, but we truly were trusting God for the outcome.

They took John back for another scan in order to determine exactly where to insert the needle. It would have to go right into his lung. I wasn't too thrilled about that.

A nurse came to take me to the area to wait with John until the scan came back. I was only back there about ten minutes when the doctor came in.

"There's no need for this biopsy," he said. "The mass had melted away. It's gone."

I threw my hands up in the air saying, "Woo Hoo! Praise Jesus!"

John was a little quieter, but he was saying, "Praise the Lord." And lifting his hand.

All the staff just stared at us. I guess they weren't used to reactions like that. John told them why we were here and what God had called us to do.

The doctor was smiling as he said, "Well, if God can wait just another minute, I'm going to get these results on a disc for you in case you should need it."

He was back shortly and we were on our way. John took a detour upstairs to tell the nurses, who had cared for him when he was sick, that God had healed him and we would be back on the road soon. They were so excited.

We had put our trust in God, and He had indeed come through. I was glad to give everyone who had been praying for us the amazing news!

I am thankful to God for all the times He gave me what I needed rather than what I asked for.

That thankfulness was on my heart all the time. And along with that came the realization that I had done what I see others doing frequently. I had tried to believe what I was hearing wasn't the voice of God, because it wasn't what I wanted to hear.

I recalled waking up months earlier to hear the Lord say this.

Words, Words, Words
All they want is another word,
When they haven't obeyed the one
I gave them yesterday!

Believe it or not, this is something I encounter frequently. People always want a word from God. But if that word doesn't suit them, by the next day they want another word from God.

I had no excuse. I know the voice of the Lord. I knew very well what God had spoken to me about being still and staying put. A friend had even called me to say, while she and her husband were praying for us, they had both heard the Lord say we were to be still. We need to be very careful about saying a word is not really God. Make sure it isn't that you just don't want to hear that particular word.

Three days later, we were heading south. Thank You, Lord, for always being so good to us.

Kentucky

The night before we left Illinois, I woke up in the middle of the night and spoke out loud the names of a couple I had met a year earlier. Had I been asked their names, I couldn't have told you their first or last name, so I knew God was speaking to me about them. As I prayed about this, God told me we were to stop and see them.

They lived in Kentucky. It was a different route than we normally would have taken, but not out of our way. After calling them, we made plans to stop there.

The day we were to meet with them, I woke up with a headache. I was thankful we didn't have to meet until evening because, by late morning, my headache was much worse.

John suggested we go get some coffee, and we ended up at a little coffee shop that was calm and quiet. After ordering coffee, we sat in the booth, both of us praying a little, just quietly. I had felt God was going to tell me something important. I cannot explain it, but sometimes when God is getting ready to impart something to me that is really important, my head will hurt terribly right before I hear the Lord speak to me. It doesn't happen often, but occasionally, and I have come to recognize that headache. I have had people try to tell me what that's about, but I still don't understand it. I only know that, after I hear what the Lord is saying to me, the headache is gone. Just completely gone!

John and I looked at each other and said it almost at the very same time.

"I believe God is saying we need to rest for the winter."

Yes! We knew God had spoken it to both of us at the very same time. And then Dauphin Island came to both of us. And within a couple of minutes the headache was gone.

You may think that wasn't necessarily a message of the utmost importance. I might have thought that, as well. However, I know that I am not a good "rester." I much prefer to be busy, doing something, all the time. And John needed to rest. That pneumonia had taken something out of him. I saw how easily he got tired and his face was still pale. John is not a complainer, but he didn't have to say anything for me to know he was not himself. And who knows, as much as I wouldn't want to admit it, maybe I needed to rest also. We had been going at a pretty good clip for almost a year and a half at this point.

The peace that comes from knowing what God wants you to do, and having it settled in your heart that you are going to do exactly what He wants you to, is an amazing thing.

We met the couple for dinner that evening. God gave us a message for them that was wonderful confirmation to a big move they were getting ready to make. They encouraged us as well.

The next day, we were back on the road. We had a very encouraging phone call from the guy we had given our minivan to. He had been blessed with another car and had passed our van on to a pastor in Mississippi who needed a vehicle. That pastor was now using the van to transport children to church. It seemed that minivan was the gift that kept on giving. Thank You, Lord, for allowing us to be a part of all that.

In early August I spoke to two ladies' groups. God gave me a special word for those ladies in addition to the message I gave almost everywhere I went.

You are to tell the ladies this,

My child.

Get your house in order.
Each one will know what this
means to them.

Get your house in order and do
it quickly.
Do not lag.
This is for your own protection
and that of your family.
Get your house in order!
The time is short!
Do not act as if you have forever
to do it.

The time is short, My child,
and they will regret it if they
do not pay heed to this warning.

Most of those ladies seemed to know right away what this word meant for them personally. I could see it in their eyes. A knowing. Almost like God had already told them and they just hadn't done it yet. A few confirmed this to me privately after the meetings. God is so great about that. He can give a word to an entire group of people, and each one gets something personal out of it. It is like He is whispering in each ear exactly what that person needed to hear.

He who dwells in the shelter of the Most High will abide in the shadow of the Almighty.

Psalm 91:1 (NASB)

Interpretation of the Dream

It was August 2nd, 3:35am. I woke up from a dream for the third time tonight. I hadn't been able to recall any of those dreams, so I had just gone back to sleep. By the third time I woke up, I felt I was having the same dream over and over, but I still didn't know what that dream was.

I lay there a few minutes, waiting on the Lord. I knew this was important somehow. Then the dream came to my mind that I had almost a year earlier. I'm sure you'll remember it. The dream where I was standing at the end of the road where the two houses had burned.

While I still wasn't sure that was what I had been dreaming about tonight, I felt in my spirit God was going to tell me something about that dream, so I got up right away with my Bible and journal. Ready to write. And God was ready to tell me some things.

The following is the interpretation of that dream. Please go back and read it if you need to refresh your memory on what that dream was about. You will find it beginning on page 121.

> *The houses, My child, represent the White House and the U.S. Capitol Building.*

The fire began in the stone house, which represented the White House.

The brick house represented the Capitol Building.

You could tell they used to be stately buildings. Not really from what you saw, but what you sensed.

They were completely empty. Everything inside had totally burned away. There was not even a trace of what used to be there.

The stone house seemed dirty to you. That's because it is. The White House hasn't been white (clean) in a long time. It was very, very dark. You had a hard time seeing what was left of it.

There was a little more of the brick house left standing, but it had succumbed to the fire as well.

The firefighters are the Church. They finally got the fire put out, but it was too late.

There was truly nothing left. Absolutely nothing inside and barely a shell of the outside.

The Church is so dejected and discouraged. They are still trying, as seen when a couple of them "came alive" long enough to warn you to get back from the fire. But, you notice, that's all they did. Nothing more.

The road, My child. The road just stopped.

Some of those firefighters should have been getting people off that road heading them in the right direction. But there was no warning from them until you came almost to the fire.

Then they tried to step forward a bit, but still not in full force.

Only a very small remnant of those firefighters were stepping forward to warn you not to continue in that direction.

And did you notice they had almost no equipment? No trucks? Just a few small hoses that were very old, almost antique looking.

The city off in the distance is the rest of the nation. It's burning, My child. Not to the point of the two houses, but burning. And the "firefighters" are not putting it out.

Very few know or care how close it is to burning down.

*I don't usually get clear
interpretations of dreams.
But this one was to be different.
A dream I'd had almost
a year ago.
And God was clearly telling me
what that dream meant.*

*And it shall be
that everyone who calls on the name of the Lord
shall be saved.*

Acts 2:21 (NASB)

A Boy and His Bible

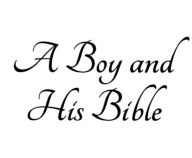

Around mid-August we left for New England, where I would speak at my son's church. We drove the car and left the motor home behind. It was so good to be with Zack and his family.

A number of people wanted to meet with John and I, to have a meal or get a cup of coffee, and talk about what the Lord was telling us. It was great to be around people who wanted to hear what the Lord was saying. John and I have been so blessed to find a remnant in every part of the country who has been very receptive to us.

This leg of the journey was similar to the others, in that God had people all along the way for us to minister to.

I remember early one morning, the Lord telling me we needed to get off the next exit and stop at McDonald's. A lady was standing at the counter next to me, placing an order, when God told me I needed to talk to her.

It didn't take long for her to tell me that she knew God, and had been raised in church, but hadn't been back for a long time. The Lord told me I needed to give her a Bible. I went out to the car to get one, and He was specific about which one she should have.

When I took the Bible back to her, she burst into tears. She had never had a "pretty" Bible before. The church she had been raised in had been very rigid and her father, though at church every Sunday, had been somewhat abusive to her. It seemed to me she didn't think she deserved a pretty Bible. I made sure she understood this was the Bible God wanted her to have. I hadn't chosen the Bible. She hugged it to her chest and then hugged me.

As we continued on down the road, I thought back to a couple of years ago when John and I were in the New England area. How God had spoken to me that we were to go into two laundromats and leave Bibles there for those who came in.

In one of those laundromats, we talked with a lady who worked there. She put the Bibles out on the counter so people could get one if they wanted it. She asked me if it was okay for her to take one of the Bibles. She said she hadn't had a Bible of her own in a long time. I told her I would bring in a special Bible for her, so John and I went back out to the car to find a nice Women's Bible to give her. She was so excited! About two days later, I knew God was directing me to go back in to see her. A young boy was standing at the window of the laundromat. The lady told me it was her son, that he was nine years old, and he had been waiting for me to come. He wanted to talk to me.

I didn't question how he knew I would be coming; I just went over to talk to him. He was very polite and told me the same thing. He had been waiting for me. He wanted to know if there was any way he could get his own Bible.

I had to restrain myself from picking him up and just squeezing him! My heart just went out to him. Think about it...he was standing at the window of the laundromat, where he walked after school and waited for his Mama to get off work, waiting for the lady to come back so he could ask her if there was any way he could get his own Bible.

"Of course," I told him.

We were leaving for Maine the next morning, so it would be a week or so before I could come back to the laundromat, but I promised him a Bible. We were out of children's Bibles or I would have given him one right then. I knew we would have to purchase a special one for that little boy.

About a week and a half later, John and I were back at the laundromat.

We had a blue Boy's Explorer Bible. It had some shiny silver on the cover. We had gone in the afternoon hoping he would be there after school again.

He was waiting for me. His mother told me the last four days he kept asking her if she thought the lady was really coming back with a Bible for him. Bless his little heart! And I wish you all could have seen his face when he saw his Bible. He hugged me and hugged me and told me he was going to read all the stories in it.

Then he said he had a sister who was a teenager. If we ever came back could we bring a Bible for her, too?

"I think she would like a pink one," he said.

We just happened to have a pink one in our box of Bibles in the car. It was perfect for a teenage girl!

I pray for them when God brings
that little family to my heart.
I don't think I'll ever forget
that little boy's face
when he saw his Bible.

If that would have been
the only stop in New England,
it would have been worth the trip.

For if you
forgive others
for their transgressions,
your heavenly Father
will also forgive you.

Matthew 6:14 (NASB)

Behind Closed Doors

It was 5:06am on August 24th and I was awake. We were still in New England. I got up to pray.

I felt a stirring. Something was going on in our nation that was unprecedented. I was on my knees, crying out to God, asking Him if He would tell me anything about what was taking place. Then I saw the doors again. I can't say for sure how many times I had seen a vision of those exact same doors. They are huge, taller and wider than other doors. Dark wood with something that looked like scrollwork at the top. This time I saw more detail than normal. I could even see the handles.

And the Lord began to tell me there was much evil going on behind those doors. He told me the doors were very real.

Then I had another vision. I could see inside that room, behind those closed doors, but my vision was very limited. All I could see was underneath a huge, long table. There were a lot men sitting around the table. The only thing I could see were their legs from the knees down. It appeared they were men because they had men's dress pants on and men's shoes. The pants and shoes were all dark in color, but they weren't all exactly alike.

What came to me was that I should pray for distraction. Any kind of a distraction. Something that would take their attention away from what they were concentrating on. And as I prayed, I saw a mouse run under that table.

I can only imagine the havoc that mouse caused. God did not allow me to see anymore. I continued to pray for awhile until I felt my intercession was finished...for now.

I know some of you will think
this sounds absolutely crazy.
Believe me, a few years ago
I would have been right there with you.
But God has taken me
so many places,
and has allowed me to see
so many things,
that I am no longer quick to think,
"That can't be God!"

After all...
If you think about it,
the Bible is full of
some pretty strange things.

Leaving New England

The remainder of my time in New England was spent with our son and his family. I had a lot of opportunities to attend meetings with other pastors, many who were meeting together to repent and pray for our nation.

All too soon, it was time to leave New England. I sometimes feel I could stay there six months and not finish everything God has for me to do. But it was time to go. The rest would have to wait for the next time.

There were a number of stops along the way as John and I drove south. There were people we needed to meet with in North Carolina and South Carolina, as well as unexpected God appointments.

Near the end of September, I woke up to the Lord saying —

Let's talk.

About what, Lord?

Everything.
About everything.
Anything.

So I took Him at His word.

I asked Him to heal my husband and make him completely whole.
I asked God to give him wisdom.

I told the Lord I wanted to hear Him so clearly, and asked for the
strength to be obedient.

For some time, I told the Lord what I wanted. Some of it sounded
so selfish.

Then I began to tell Him what I wanted for our nation, the world
– everybody, everywhere.

And now Lord, what do you want from me?

I want you to be faithful to spend
time with Me, My child.

I want you to be a good witness in
every way, to everyone.
I want you to live your life that way.

I want you to share what I've given you.

Spend more time in My word.

Hesitate before making decisions.
Come to Me and I will help you
make them.

Be generous.

Enjoy all that I've given you.

I love you, My child.
Now go back to bed.

My friend,
I wouldn't trade
that relationship with the Lord
for anything
this world has to offer.

Resting for the Winter

John and I hadn't been able to get reservations at the campground on Dauphin Island, Alabama, but we still believed God had said that was where we were supposed to rest for the winter.

In early October we were in Knoxville, packing the motor home with supplies and preparing to leave at a moment's notice, should we find out they had a spot for us.

I received a call from the pastor's wife on the island. The Lord had told her to call the campground. She had called immediately and was told they just had a cancelation. She told them to hold it for us and we would call right away. I called them and took the camping spot. Once again, we had trusted God and He came through for us.

John and I were on our way to Dauphin Island when we received a phone call about hurricane warnings in the gulf. We stopped at a rest stop to pray. Feeling we needed to hold off for a couple of days until we saw what the weather was like, we drove a couple of exits down the highway to stop in a Walmart parking lot. We decided to park there for the night and see where God would lead us after that.

It was here where God would lead me to another Waffle House and another divine appointment.

Charlie

We unhooked the car near evening and drove around just checking out the area. There was a Waffle House nearby. I had a strong sense we needed to go, but I didn't feel the time was quite right, so I told John maybe we would go later.

Later that afternoon, I knew it was time to go to that Waffle House. John and I went in, found a booth, and sat down to order.

When the waitress brought our food, I asked her if she needed prayer for anything. She smiled, thanked us for asking, and told us what she wanted prayer for. That seemed important, but I didn't feel that's what God had brought us in here for.

A few minutes later, an older gentleman came in pulling an oxygen tank along behind him. He sat down on the first stool at the counter. I was drawn to him and watched as he placed his order. I could tell he was a regular when the cook and waitresses all began to chat with him as they walked past where he was sitting.

A short time later, I was telling John I needed to talk to that man. Walking to the counter I sat down next to him and introduced myself.

He said, "Well, I'm Charlie."

After a bit of small talk, I asked if he knew Jesus as his personal Savior. Looking into his twinkling eyes, I felt I already knew the answer to that, but still needed to ask.

He said, "I sure do, young lady. Until I got where I couldn't breathe good I used to play the guitar and sing at church. I don't do that anymore. I just don't have enough breath left in me."

I inquired about his church, telling him if my husband and I were still in the area we would go there on Sunday. He told me the name of it and gave me some brief directions.

The next day, we located a nice campground in the area where we could stay until the hurricane warnings were over.

Sunday morning found us at Charlie's church. We arrived a few minutes early. Charlie was already there, up front practicing with the praise team. I hadn't really expected him to be there, much less playing and singing, but there he was. I could tell all the regulars were so glad to see him.

As John and I introduced ourselves, we found out that Charlie had already told them about meeting us and that we would be coming. He didn't seem to have any doubts about whether or not this strange lady who came up to talk to him in Waffle House would actually show up at his church on Sunday. I was so glad we had made the effort to find this little church way out in the country.

We were asked to share about our ministry, which we did, and also told them how we had met Charlie.

The church was quite small and there was such a sweet spirit there. We really enjoyed the music and recognized Charlie was quite an asset to their praise team. He had obviously been playing and singing for a long, long time. You could tell it came so natural to him.

At the end of the service, some people came up to speak with us, and by the time we were free, we didn't see Charlie anywhere. We left, knowing God had indeed sent us to worship with those people at that little church. But most of all, God had sent us into that Waffle House to speak with Charlie and give him one more Sunday morning to play and sing.

Sometime I would like to stop at that Waffle House to inquire about him. I'm sure the employees would know who I was talking about. Charlie may well be playing and singing in Heaven by now, but I thank God that John and I had the blessing of getting to hear him play and sing here on earth.

John and I continued on to Dauphin Island. They had gotten a lot of wind and rain from the hurricane, but no real damage.

John did a good job of resting; I can't say the same for myself. I did rest some, but everywhere I went people needed ministering to, and it seemed God opened doors all over. From the couple who just felt they should invite us to share their gazebo at the coffee shop, to people all over the campground, God never ceased to put someone in front of us who needed to hear from God, about God, or needed us to pray for them.

As you will see in the following section, we must be very cautious about how to proceed when we meet people with whom we feel led to minister to. God may indeed have sent them to you, or not. Either way, we must always listen for His voice to know what to do, and be careful not to get ahead of Him.

How Easily We Are Deceived

Oh no, we think. Not me. And yet it's so easy to be deceived. The Bible warns us over and over again saying, *'Do not be deceived... let no man deceive you... even the very elect would be deceived...for sin deceived me...'* But even after all this, we actually believe it could not happen to us. I believe in this season, God is allowing us to encounter situations where we see how easily we can be deceived into believing something is not only good or right, but that it is actually from God. This happened to my husband and I recently.

While fishing at a pier, John met some ladies who had come there to take pictures. Hearing one of them make some comments about God, he began to talk with them. He shared a little with them about our ministry. A couple of days later, one of the ladies stopped by the campground to meet me. I wasn't there, so she left her card. After we had emailed each other and then spoke on the phone, she expressed a desire to meet me. She felt we had a lot in common. She was a publisher, I an author, and we both believed in divine appointments. John and I were invited to come by a house where she was staying. Some friends of hers would be there as they all belonged to a travel club and would be having a short meeting. She had to leave the next day, so this was the only opportunity we would have to meet each other and talk for a bit. I didn't totally commit to the meeting, but told her I thought we could make it. I wasn't completely settled in my spirit about going but figured we could always just leave if we didn't like things after we got there.

There were a few couples at the house and everyone welcomed us. A couple of the ladies drew me in right away, asking about the ministry, wanting to know about my book (*From Our Wicked Ways*), and even asking to purchase a copy. They wanted to hear all about God speaking to me, what He was saying, etc., etc. I sat at the table and shared different things, soon realizing everyone had stopped talking and they were all listening intently. Never wanting to miss an opportunity to talk about what God is doing, I answered questions and talked for quite awhile.

They were all extremely nice, and by their conversation, John and I soon realized we were in a group of people who loved God. I'm sure we let our guard down possibly more than we should have, and certainly more than we normally would. We allowed ourselves to be lulled into a false sense of security.

Finally, someone said there was a short presentation they wanted to show us and would we move over to the sofa. We did and a man put a DVD in his laptop. We quickly became aware we were the focus of the meeting and had been invited here in hopes that we would join the travel club. The entire presentation, DVD, and a few of them sharing their stories about how they became involved in this, lasted close to an hour.

The more we heard, the better it sounded, and the check in my spirit, that had been there even before we accepted the invitation to join them, was growing fainter.

It was some sort of a pyramid where you paid a certain amount to join, and then a small monthly payment until you got a certain number of people under you. Then there would be no more payments and you would soon be earning money. All the while enjoying very inexpensive trips to places all over the world.

Some people even used their trip points to travel for their ministry and go on mission trips. The club itself does mission trips where they build schools and do other humanitarian work. There are pastors and missionaries who are part of the club as well.

As we all talked, I thought back to the prophetic word we had received in late February 2013 about how this Thanksgiving would truly be a time of thanksgiving for John and I. Quite possibly, this could be the blessing God had planned for us. After all, He uses all sorts of venues to carry out His plans. We really felt this might be for us. There wasn't a lot of money required from us and the payoff sounded great, although we knew it would be a little while before we would see that. We did at least have the wisdom to tell them we would have to pray and talk about it, but felt we might be joining their club.

Both of us were excited as we headed to the car. It wasn't until we actually got into the car and closed the doors that I was aware of the check in my spirit. I'm not sure if it was there all the time and I had ignored it, or if God waited until we got in the car and closed the doors to alert me to the fact that all was not quite as we thought it was.

By the time we got back to the campground, I was feeling irritated. This entire thing just didn't seem to fit the plan, the God-orchestrated plan that He had been guiding us through for the past few years. To begin with, it felt like a job of sorts, and I knew God had taken me out of my secular job more than six years ago. Anytime I began to think about getting another job, He was very quick to remind me that was not His plan.

Then John delivered the clincher. "How can you try to get people to join this travel club while delivering the words God has given you? I'm just not sure it fits," he said.

It was like putting the piece in the puzzle that enables you to really see what the picture looks like. I knew he was right. There was no way I could deliver the message of repentance, judgment, preparation, and hope while saying 'but wouldn't you like to join this travel club, do some traveling, earn a car and make money?'

How did I not see that from the start? How could I have been deceived enough to even entertain the idea of being a part of this?

I thought back to when I sensed something was not right about this, and I realized it was just after we shut the car doors. What came to my mind was that we had shut out the noise and closed ourselves in with God. Sort of like going into your prayer closet to get alone with the Lord. Often, that's what we need to do in order to truly hear what God is saying to us. It is necessary to get to a place of privacy with Him, shut out all distraction, and just listen. He will be faithful to reveal to each one of us what the truth really is about a situation.

I knew before we even went to bed that we would not be joining any travel club. I'm not saying there was anything wrong with the club. It might be fine for the ones we had met. Possibly even a huge blessing to some. But it was not for us. The mandate God has on our lives would not allow any room for something like that.

I repented for even considering it. Asking for quicker discernment and more wisdom I headed off to bed, thanking God He had protected us from actually becoming involved in something that was not His plan for our lives.

I pray for those people as the Lord brings them to my mind. They were all so kind to us. I believe God intended for our paths to cross, but it is possible John and I were never supposed to go to that meeting.

Ministry at Every Turn

It was almost time to leave the island for Christmas. We would be spending the holidays with our children and grandchildren, then returning for the remainder of the winter.

We had rested, John more than I, but the ministry opportunities were endless. I had preached at the Methodist church, spoken to small groups, and given out Bibles wherever the Lord led. We had given bags of Bibles to a couple who ministered to the homeless.

I recall one Bible in particular. It was pink and waterproof. The pages felt like thin plastic. As I was putting Bibles in the bag for this couple, the Holy Spirit clearly spoke to me that I was to include that one. I found out a couple of days later how God used that Bible.

This couple had gone into Mobile, Alabama, with hot food, clothing, and other things for the homeless people there. A big, tall man had come up to the table to get a Bible and immediately grabbed the pink one. The lady told him he could have whichever one he wanted, and offered him one that looked a little more like a man's Bible.

Then he told her the story. Although he tried to protect his Bible, it had gotten soaked recently and the pages stuck together. He had prayed for a Bible that was waterproof!

"Now," he said with a big smile, "I can start preaching again!" It didn't bother him in the least bit that it was pink.

> *John and I have been*
> *giving out Bibles for years.*
> *Maybe one day*
> *I'll write a book on the*
> *destinations of some of those Bibles.*

A few days later, we were getting ready to leave the campground. I was inside getting things in place, and John was outside unhooking the water and electricity.

There was a couple parked in the camping spot next to ours. They had been there for about a week. John and I had talked to them briefly a few times.

The man came out of their camper and headed toward the motor home to say good-bye. I slid open the window and screen over our couch and leaned out to tell them bye.

I asked how much longer they would be staying and the man wasn't sure, telling me his wife needed a break. She was struggling with some things. At that point, she came out and walked over to where her husband was standing. He continued to talk to me about some things that had been going on with them and she joined in.

I immediately recognized a lot of demonic activity. Not necessarily on their part, but on other people who were around them a lot. So I gave them a crash course in deliverance as I hung out the window.

I taught them about breaking ungodly soul ties, spiritually cleaning their house and not allowing certain things in, even if it offends other people.

I talked to him about covering his wife and protecting her. She began to sob and he was wiping tears, too.

I don't know how long I leaned out that window ministering to that couple. They were precious, and I knew they were soaking in what I was telling them. A few times I thought about going outside, but was concerned that might be just enough of a distraction to cause a disconnect somehow. So I stayed at the window.

Finally, it wound to a close and, after I prayed for them, John and I pulled out.

But everyone who calls
on the name of the Lord will be saved

Joel 2:32a (NLT)

Dancing with Allen

I believe it's only fitting for me to close out 2013 with a Waffle House story. This took place in mid-December.

A good friend wanted to take me out to dinner. She suggested we go to a restaurant she knew I would like. I told her that was fine and arranged to meet her there.

The Waffle House kept coming to my mind and I just pushed it away, knowing I was supposed to meet Dawn. It just kept coming back and I knew it was God. While I was thinking I should call her and ask if we could change our meeting place, she called me. She had been feeling like we should go somewhere different. I told her what kept coming to my mind and that I felt it was God. Being one who is sensitive to what the Lord is saying, that was all she needed to hear.

There was only one table left when we arrived. It amazes me how busy Waffle House is at all hours of the night and day. We sat down and ordered, but my eyes were roving and my heart and mind were tuned in to listen for the Holy Spirit.

I kept going back to a man who was sitting with a blonde lady, all the way at the other end of the restaurant. There was nothing terribly unusual about them, but I continued to be drawn there.

Dawn and I had finished eating, and we were drinking our coffee and catching up on what God had been doing with our lives, when the man got up and came back to the jukebox, which was really close to our booth. I could tell he was having a problem. He couldn't figure out how to make it work. Finally, he turned around to me and asked if I could help him.

I got up and read the directions on the front of the jukebox. It was a new model and to be honest, it was a little confusing, but I helped him get it going. I sat back down, but he wanted to talk.

He stepped over to our table, said his name was Allen, and he wanted to thank me. Then he asked me to dance! I could tell he had probably been drinking and I tried to ignore him. There was no ignoring him! He continued to ask me to dance.

I kept telling him no, and finally I said, "Look. I'm a Chaplain. I'm not going to get up and dance with you in the Waffle House or anywhere else." I'm not sure what I thought being a Chaplain had to do with it, but I had gotten his attention. He wanted to talk about me being a Chaplain.

The lady he was with must have gotten tired of waiting for him, because she headed for the door. He ran off to stop her and talked her into sitting back down at their table. But within five minutes he was back.

He said he just felt like he needed to talk to me. I knew it was God and that Allen was the reason I was having dinner at the Waffle House instead of the other restaurant I especially liked.

So I didn't invite him to sit down, but I did decide to talk to him. And talk we did! About everything from his ex-wife (who he wanted me to call and talk to about God because she was a psychic), to his drinking, and about how far away from home he was. He had come into town on business. I just let him talk.

He put some more money in the jukebox and, although he chose the songs, I had to help him push the right buttons again to get it to play. Interesting...this time he played two contemporary Christian songs along with the rest. He said he thought I might like those. I was surprised to find Christian music was one of the choices and that he even knew the titles of those songs.

The lady got up to leave again and he ran to the door to coax her into sitting back down again.

It was looking like a three-ring circus. Dawn and I wanted to laugh, but we both knew God wasn't finished with this.

Pretty soon, Allen was back. This time, I sensed it was my turn to do most of the talking and, to his credit, he listened. I told him my friend and I were supposed to go to another restaurant, but God had brought us here because we were supposed to talk to him. He accepted that pretty well. I talked to him about his life and how he had gotten to where he was. He tried to tell me some things, and then I asked him if he wanted to tell me the truth now. And he did.

I wanted him to understand that Almighty God had really sent me to the Waffle House because of him. I was silently asking the Lord to give me the words to help him understand the significance of that.

Finally, I asked if he knew Jesus as his personal Savior.

"Once I did," he told me. "But I guess not now."

I told him how easy it was to turn back to God. How he doesn't have to wait until he cleans himself up or until he is in church, but that God will take him back at anytime, anywhere.

His eyes seemed to light up at that.

"I need to do that," he said. "I need to do it soon."

"Yes, you do, Allen."

He didn't want to pray right then and that was okay. He had sobered up enough to thank me sincerely for talking to him about the Lord. Then he went back to sit down with the blonde.

A few minutes later, he came back with a piece of paper. He had written his ex-wife's name and phone number down and wanted me to call and talk to her. I told him I would certainly pray about it.

He seemed a little disappointed until I said, "I don't do much of anything without praying about it first."

He said he understood.

He went back to his table and a short while later he waved at me as they got up to leave. I walked to the door, asked if I could pray for them before they left. They both said I could. So I stood between the two double doors, held their hands, and prayed for them. Then I watched them walk off into the night.

John and I would be with our family in just a few days to celebrate Christmas. I had no idea where Allen or his friend would be spending Christmas. I wondered if it would be just another day for them. I continued to look out the door, asking the Lord to make Himself real to them. So real their lives would be forever changed.

I pray Allen doesn't ever forget
the conversation that took place
in that Waffle House.
I pray he always remembers
that God loved him enough
to send someone to meet him there.
And I pray, if he hasn't done so already,
that he turns his heart back
to the Lord very soon.

January 2014

I woke up early today and asked God what the word was for this year. I don't do this every January 1st, but I did today. Do you know what He said to me?

Be thankful!

That's it. Two words. But two words we don't use often enough.

Then, on January 11 at 2:30am, He continued to speak to me about thankfulness. I believe each one of us needs to put a copy of this word on our refrigerator to remind us of this every day. This is what the Lord said —

> **You must listen carefully.**
> **I am giving you a new word of great importance.**
> **One people haven't heard from you before.**
>
> **Listen, My child.**
> **Get it down carefully.**
>
> **People must be thankful. Thankful. Thankful.**
> **It must be their new way of life.**
>
> **If they want to hold on to what they are thankful for,**
> **They must begin to speak it out.**
> **Cry it out to Me.**

I want to hear of their thankfulness.

I want to hear a cry of thankfulness shout up from the earth as never before in history!
I want to hear it loud and clear. Every day!
Everywhere! From everyone!
I must hear it! As a chorus!
They must speak it out.
It needs to be the subject of the day. Every day.

Let's not talk about what's coming.
Let's talk about your thankfulness.
Write it! Speak it! Shout it! Yes!!
Thankfulness will fill the skies.

The enemy will be thwarted, confused, and confounded!

Let it begin!

What an amazing word to begin 2014 with! Dauphin Island United Methodist Church was the first place this word was given and everyone wanted a copy.

However, we found that everywhere this word was given, people lined up to get a copy of it. I pray they took it seriously and are thanking the Lord, not just daily, but many times a day, for *everything*. So often we only thank Him for what we consider the big things, forgetting that it is only by God's grace that we take our next breath.

Thank You, Lord,
for loving us unconditionally,
for showing us grace
when we don't deserve it.
Thank You, Lord,
for protecting us
when we didn't even realize
we were in danger.
Thank You, Lord,
for providing everything we need,

and much of what we want.
Thank You, Lord,
for waking us up this morning.
Thank You, Lord,
for giving us that next breath.
Thank You, Lord.

Choices

Mid January found us back at the campground in Dauphin Island where John would rest for the remainder of the winter, and I would try to. I did rest there. It was restful just to be stationary for a while.

We met a couple with a young daughter who had come to stay at the campground while we had been away for Christmas. They shared how they had lost everything.   Jobs, their home, everything. For a couple of years now, they had been living in an RV, traveling around to different parts of the country. He was doing odd jobs wherever something was available to support his family. Churches would occasionally take up donations for them as well.

While my heart went out to them, I sensed a tremendous amount of bitterness.   And there was certainly enough blame to go around a few times.

John and I were strongly led to reach out to them. We talked with them, prayed with them, and brought them bags and bags of groceries and treats for the little girl. They were all precious.

They were attending the same church we were while staying at the campground, and one morning the Lord spoke to me clearly about what I was to say to this man. So before Sunday School began I went to the table they were sitting at to talk with him. I simply asked if he had ever asked Jesus into his heart.

He said, "No ma'am, I haven't."

He had shown me different times all the things he had written concerning scripture, and he carried a large, well-worn Bible. It seemed as though he had written and studied enough to be a Bible scholar. Everyone thought he had received salvation by the way he talked. But God knew differently, so he sent me to ask the man outright.

After his response, I asked him if he wanted to accept the Lord. He told me he did not. I was a little surprised and asked him why. He began to tell me about how horrible his childhood was and that his parents had given him up because of their lifestyle.

Then he said, "Why would I want to accept a God who would take my parents from me and allow me to go through such a horrible life?"

Whoa! I looked him in the eyes and lovingly but firmly spoke.

"God did not take your parents away from you. Your parents made choices. It sounds like those choices hurt you terribly, but you cannot blame God for the choices your parents made." I let that sink in for a moment. "Nor can you blame God for the choices you are making that are going to affect your daughter for the rest of her life. You'd better think about that."

He was silent. I knew those words had hit their mark.

I hugged him and said, "John and I are here for you if you need to talk."

A few days later we stopped by their RV on our way to the store, to see if they needed bread and milk. They were very discouraged. The campground was full with reservations so they would have to leave in two days. The man was even blaming the people in the office because the campground was booked up.

We talked and prayed with them extensively. Nothing seemed to have the desired results, but we had to leave that with the Lord.

They came to say good-bye and to thank us the morning they were pulling out. Our hearts broke for that little family. All we could do was love on them and hope they could see Jesus in us.

John and I were once again
reminded of
"the wake"
our son-in-law had seen
behind us.
We are all only responsible
for continuing to move forward
in whatever God has called us to do.
Never knowing,
only trusting,
for the miraculous to happen
in the "wake of the Holy Spirit."

Let's talk for a moment about choices. I hadn't intended to include this story in the book, but it seemed God wouldn't let me leave it out, so that must mean there is someone out there who needs to read it.

All of us have so many choices to make each and every day. Some are small and don't seem to make much difference to us. Some seem small, but are actually much bigger than we realize, and will affect more people than we think they will. And then there are the really important choices.

The most important choice you will ever make is to accept Jesus as your Savior. That is an eternal choice. Even if we live to be 100, the amount of time we will have spent on this earth is still only a speck compared with the time we will spend in eternity.

There are other important choices we must make as well. I won't go into a list of those. They are different for each of us. I will just say we need to think about how our choices affect other people, not just whether they suit us for the moment.

Draw
near to
God
and
He will
draw
near
to you.

James 4:8 (NASB)

Back On the Road

The winter was over, and we knew it was time to get back on the road. After leaving Dauphin Island, we drove east on I-10. We had just gotten into Florida when I grabbed a napkin off the dash to write down what I was hearing the Lord say.

> **God wants to revive this place once again.**
> **He wants to put His handprint here**
> **once again.**
> **He wants to bring beauty out of ashes**
> **and revive the fire.**
> **But the focus *must* remain on Him**
> **and on unity,**
> **not on the things that divide.**

"What am I supposed to do with this, Lord?"

Take it to Brownsville Assembly of God.

It was so clear. I copied the word exactly as God had spoken it to me into my journal, then again on a sheet of paper to give to the pastor there.

We arrived at Brownsville Assembly in Pensacola, and went inside to locate a pastor. The girl at the desk told us the Senior Pastor wasn't in, but she went to get another one of their pastors. She didn't seem at all put off when we told her we had a word from the Lord for the pastor, and neither did the pastor when he came out to greet us.

I spoke the word to him and gave him the paper I had written it on. He thanked us and talked about how others had been hearing similar things, and they were putting things in motion as the Lord was directing. Then he prayed anointing and protection over us, and for the blood of Jesus to cover us. John and I could tell he was praying as the Holy Spirit was leading him. Greatly appreciative of the prayer, we got back on the road.

We had been driving a few hours when some guys in a Jeep came up beside us and tried to get us to pull over. There was a gravel area where we could have stopped, but John continued to drive. After realizing we weren't going to pull over, they tried to run us off the road! There were four or five men in the Jeep. As they continued to move toward the side of the motor home and then swerve out again, John stepped on the gas and pulled away from them. They pulled off into the gravel area and we continued on down the road.

I don't know what was going on with those guys, but we were thankful that pastor had plead the blood of Jesus and prayed protection over us.

Feeling compelled not to pull off anywhere, we continued on until we reached Columbia, South Carolina, where we are so blessed to have a church where we can park the motor home with all the hook-ups we need. Not only is the parking spot such a blessing, but the church treats us like family. We love being there. As John was outside getting things hooked up for the motor home, we looked up and saw the cross almost right over our heads. John and I both felt covered and protected as we settled in for the night.

I recall, when we first went on the road, our son said he saw us like Paul. God would send us to particular areas to preach and speak words from God, and then later we would go back to those areas to speak again and sometimes just to encourage people. I didn't see that whole picture when Zack first said that, but as time has gone by, I am seeing it more and more. Columbia is one of those places God sends us back to again and again. I believe it is two-fold there. We encourage the remnant there and bring them what the Lord is telling us, and they encourage and love on us. That area is the biggest financial support to the ministry as well. We have made so many close friends there and we thank the Lord for them.

On this particular trip to Columbia, we met with different groups to pray with them and share what God was saying to us. The word on thankfulness seemed to be a great encouragement and a big hit everywhere we went. The phrase that comes to me is "a lifter up of heads." That word just seemed to bring a light to their eyes and people literally lifted up their heads upon hearing it.

We also brought a warning about not being deceived and lulled into a false sense of security. We need to be alert at all times.

There was quite an ice storm during the time we were in Columbia. Our motor home was just about encased in ice and we were unable to go anywhere. The worst of it only lasted two days. We were thankful for that, but realized later that, as the ice melted, water had gotten into the motor home somehow. The wall and carpet were quite wet and it took quite a bit of work to get it dried out.

John and I knew we were coming to a place where a newer motor home was going to be necessary if we were to continue to stay on the road. We prayed about it often, just bringing our requests to the Lord. We didn't want to complain, because we were very thankful for what God had given us.

It was around the time we were leaving Columbia when God began to speak to me about a mission He was going to send me on. He wasn't giving me a lot of details about it, but that wasn't unusual. Often, we didn't know where God would send us until the day before we were to leave.

This seemed different somehow. Almost like an undercover operation of some sort. God continued to caution me about talking to more than just John and one or two very close confidants.

As we stopped in Hickory, North Carolina, on our way through, a lady called and invited me to dinner. I know her well, but she had never before called me. I only had one evening open. Feeling this was a "God-meeting" I agreed to meet her that evening. We talked about what the Lord had been speaking to each of us, sort of comparing notes. There was a lot of similarity in what God was saying to us. It is always good to get confirmation. As we were preparing to leave, she handed me an envelope and said that God had told her exactly what she was to do. I thanked her and we went our separate ways.

It was a while later before I felt I was supposed to open the envelope. When I did, I found a card and five $100 bills inside. It was then that God spoke to me more about the mission He would be sending me on.

> **You are to use only cash**
> **on this trip.**
> **You need to be very careful**
> **not to tell too many people**
> **what you are doing.**
> **You will be going by yourself.**

This was getting stranger all the time. I knew it was God telling me these things, but this would definitely be different from what we were used to.

I wasn't sure about the timing for this journey, but I knew God would let me know when I was to go.

I had intended to write more
about this mission
later in the book,
but God did not give me
the liberty to write anything
more about it.

Suffice it to say,
God did take me on this mission
and the mission was accomplished.

Churches

Lawrenceburg, Tennessee

Lawrenceburg, Tennessee...My birthplace.
I lived here until I was almost 7,
then we moved north, my mother and I.
We have come back regularly over the years to visit
family.
It's interesting how when a person is young there is no interest, or
very little, in things of your past. I think back on all those years
when I came here, and thought how boring it was to drive past
places we lived, and visit people my mother and aunt knew "way
back then."
Today, I would give much to have all that information recorded
somehow; notes, pictures, even an audio recording.
But that of course is not to be.
So here I am, knowing God has brought me here, but
unsure why.
Here I am, going through archived city directories that
are 50+ years old, talking to people, trying to get whatever
information I can.
Then my precious husband is slowly, carefully, driving
me past schools, houses, empty lots, and other places that might be
of interest to me.
He's quiet, my husband.
Understanding I am searching for something, although
I'm not sure what.
Yet both of us knowing God will show me

what that something is
before I leave this place.

Just a few days before we came here, God began to put Lawrenceburg on my mind. I hesitated, unsure of why He would send me here. So I prayed...until I was certain we were to come.

On our second night in Lawrenceburg, I woke up at 2:28am and felt I needed to get up immediately. I took my Bible and journal out to the table and didn't even have time to start praying. I heard the Lord and it sounded like He was singing.

> **The storm is coming.**
> **The storm is coming.**
> **It will wipe the land clean,**
> **wipe the land clean.**

I had heard this before from Him. The very same song.

"The song again, Lord."
I wondered if there would be more
to that song in the months to come.

We camped at David Crockett State Park for the duration of our stay in this area. After spending some time at the archives, library, and the local board of education, I was wondering what I was really doing here. It's true, I found information I hadn't known before, but what all that meant on God's calendar I wasn't totally sure of. Then I awakened in the night. God was speaking to me. He led me to read Jeremiah 18, then told me I would be speaking to some pastors; that I would warn them to warn their people. I prayed for quite some time and waited quietly to see if there was more, but that seemed to be all God had to tell me for the time being.

Around noon, I felt led to go downtown to the square. I walked around by myself and prayed.

Finally, I just asked God, "What do You want me to do?"

Very clearly I heard in that still, small voice —

Look straight ahead.
Do you see that church?
Start there.

I walked back to the car where John was waiting for me and we drove the block or so to the church. It was a large church and we drove around looking for the office. After locating it, I walked up to the door to find a bell and an intercom. After pushing the button for the intercom, a pleasant voice asked if she could help me. I asked if I could speak with the pastor. She politely told me he wasn't in and wouldn't be in all the following day, but could she take a message for him? I declined to leave a message and, thanking her I walked away. A strange coldness had settled over me. It was 77 degrees outside and the sun was shining, but I had goose bumps from the cold I was feeling. Is this the church? Is this what God intended the church to be? To speak to a faceless voice, however pleasant, through an intercom? I know many churches are using an intercom now, and I also know there are sensible reasons for it. However, today it felt so cold to me.

We drove on and shortly God directed me to stop at another church. I walked to the door marked "Office." A sign was posted "Knock for Admittance." I knocked. No one answered, so I knocked again and waited. Still no answer. I felt dread come over me as I walked back to the car. Was God showing me a picture of what the church has become? I had a strong feeling the answer to that question was "yes," but still hoping I was wrong.

The next church was a few blocks away. It was obvious these churches were handpicked by God, as we passed churches in between and I felt no leading from the Lord to stop at those. Just these three. Although I didn't know at the time this would be my last stop for the day.

Once again, the office was difficult to locate. After driving around the buildings, I found a lady who told me where I could find the pastor. I wonder if the leadership, church board, or planning committee - whoever makes the decisions regarding where the church office will be located – recognizes how hard it is for the average person to even find the office.

Once inside, a very kind lady went to get the pastor. He greeted me in a friendly manner, inviting me to come up to his office. He said he would have cleaned things up a bit if he would have known I was coming, but I thought his office looked just fine.

I began by briefly sharing how my husband and I are traveling across the country, calling America back to God. I shared how God directs me to stop and speak with pastors, and others, giving them a word from the Lord.

"That is why I am here," I say, "to bring you a word from the Lord."

Now mind you, at this precise moment I have no idea
what that word is.
I am trusting God
to speak it into my spirit at just the right time.
He has never let me down,
and I am not expecting Him to leave me hanging today.

I watch the pastor's lips twitch a bit and I realize he thinks I am some kind of quack.

"And what exactly would that word be?" he says.

Sure enough, right on time, God speaks to me.

There is a huge disaster coming to this nation.
You need to prepare your people.

I delivered the word to him exactly as the Lord had spoken it to me.

He asks a logical question. "What kind of disaster?"

I have to tell him that I have no idea. His response is rather surprising.

"Then I guess I have no idea how to prepare."

He went on to tell me that he has a big book called the Bible that tells him everything he needs to know and he doesn't need someone who hears voices coming to give him a message from God.

> *Well, I wouldn't have described myself as*
> *someone who "hears voices."*
> *It would have been very easy to get up*
> *and walk out about then,*
> *but I knew God wasn't finished with this meeting.*
> *I was very calm as I sat there.*

He wanted to know if it is an audible voice that I hear. I tell him there has only been one time, many years ago, when I heard God speak in an audible voice.

He replies, "Then how do you hear these voices?"

I say, "It is One voice that I hear, and often I wake up in the night with a strong sense that I need to get up and pray. I sit down with my Bible and journal, reading, praying, and writing what the Lord speaks to me."

"What religion are you?" he says. I tell him my husband and I are Mennonite. He compares this to the Amish, then says, "I suppose you believe all that charismatic stuff about the baptism in the spirit and all that stuff that was for the early church."

"We believe the Bible in it's entirety, from cover to cover. And we do not believe those things were just for the early church but for us today as well."

Then the pastor asked if I always hear the same message?

"No, sir." I told him. But in the past few years the Lord has given me many messages along the same vein.

Feeling led by the Lord to do so, I shared with him the word God had given me to take to the pastors in Hickory, North Carolina, in 2008.

"That proves my point!" he said. "All I need to know about repenting I can get from the Bible."

"Yes, sir. That's true. But sometimes people need to be reminded," I replied.

"The pastor is the one to do the reminding," he said.

"Sometimes the pastors need to be reminded," I responded.

He was quiet.

At that point the Holy Spirit let me know it was time for me to leave. I had done what the Lord had sent me in there to do.

I simply said, "Thank you for your time." as I rose to leave.

"Is that all you wanted?" the pastor asked.

"Yes, sir. That's all I wanted," I told him.

He continued to question me about what I really came to see him for. Finally, I thanked him again and turned toward the door.

"I'll escort you out," he said. The pastor walked behind me all the way down the stairs, through two rooms and shut the front door behind me.

As I got back into the car, I told John, "I think I prefer the locked doors and the intercom."

> *Would it have been that difficult*
> *to have simply said something like,*
> *"I'm not sure I understand all of this,*
> *however, I will certainly pray about it.*
> *Thank you for coming."*

God did not direct me to go to any more churches today. I don't know if He will send me to speak to any more pastors before I leave this area. We will just wait and see. Although these were three churches in one small town, I truly believe God was showing me a picture that resembles many churches today. I realize not all churches or pastors fall into one of these categories, and yet it is a travesty if even one does.

But if you truly obey his voice
and do all that I say,
then I will be an enemy to your enemies
and an adversary to your adversaries.

Exodus 23:22 (NASB)

The Message

It was now April and, since shortly after the beginning of the year, I had been struggling with the words God was giving me.

I kept telling Him, "God, no one wants to hear about judgment and destruction."

Those are hard words. Hard to hear and hard to give out. I asked God a number of times if there was a "better" word He could give me.

Honestly,
I had been giving a message
of repentance, judgment, and destruction
for over six years now!
I was seeing close friends
and even some family members,
withdraw and mock me.
Financial support
was declining.

The message was always
the same,
and people weren't seeing
things change.
They still had their homes,
their cars,

and money.
And they simply didn't want
to hear that things were
going to change.

It wasn't as though God
hadn't warned me.
He had.
Many times.
But I knew He also
understood my struggle.

John and I were invited to a Perry Stone Conference by a good friend. Jonathan Cahn was speaking the first night. He had only been speaking for about five minutes when God spoke to me so clearly.

The message I gave him
has never changed.
Why should yours?

"Oh God, I'm so sorry for complaining about the message You've given me. I won't do it again."

God used that conference to give me a new urgency to get that message out. He also used it to help some others have a better understanding of our ministry.

Another friend who had attended the conference came up to me after the service. She hugged and hugged me.

Then she said, "Thank you for all you do."

She continued to cry and tell me how it wasn't until she heard Jonathan Cahn speak, that she really understood what John and I were called to do.

I was so thankful to have peace about the message God had given me. It allowed me to walk in a new authority for what God had called me to do.

On April 27th at 2:45am, just over 48 hours after hearing Jonathan Cahn speak, God woke me up. I sensed an urgency and didn't waste any time getting up. God spoke to me before I even got to the living room.

My child, it's coming.

At the same time, I saw a train engine flying towards me. It was huge! Bearing down upon me. It was flying! The headlight was almost in my face. It was so big! The train was coming around a curve off to my left. It came so close that I almost flinched, all the while knowing it was a vision and not a real train. The noise was deafening. It was thundering down the tracks. But the whistle wasn't blowing.

Then it was gone.

I realized the headlight hadn't been on and the whistle wasn't blowing. I somehow knew that meant we wouldn't have the usual warning signals before our nation experiences destruction.

I was overcome by that vision. I knelt down and started to repent. But God spoke to me.

I didn't wake you up to repent.
You are up because I have things
to tell you.

You must tell people how close it is.
Tell them if there is anything
they need to do – spiritually —
they had better take care of it.

If there is someone they've
been meaning to witness to —
They need to do it now!
Do not delay!

If there is a pet sin in their life —
Get rid of it now!

THERE IS NO MORE TIME!

Wait, listen, be alert, draw near.

Tell the people to
WAKE UP! WAKE UP!

It sounded as if God was screaming this wake-up call.

It was shortly after when God spoke this to me.

> **My child, you will speak to fewer people,**
> **but they will count for more,**
> **because they will be handpicked by Me.**

Missouri

During this time, the Lord began to speak to me about Missouri. A friend of mine lived there at one time, but I hadn't heard from her in seven or eight years and I didn't even have a current phone number for her. Not that it's necessary to have a contact person, as God certainly showed us in the trip out west, but having a contact is helpful when you're going into unknown territory.

Just a couple of weeks before we were leaving for Missouri, I received a phone call. Of course, you already know who was on the other end of that phone. It was my friend, Gina, who I hadn't spoken to in such a long time. My cell phone number had remained the same all these years. God had really put me on her heart, and then she found my number on a piece of paper. God is so faithful to make those divine connections and give confirmation at the same time.

We headed for Missouri, with a stop in Memphis, Tennessee, to speak to a group who had asked us to come. It was good that we had left early in the morning before it got too hot, because our generator wouldn't stay running and that was the only way we had any air conditioning while we were traveling.

After arriving in Memphis, we met with the couple who had invited us to come. They took us to lunch and, at one point, the man turned to me and asked, "What is the Lord telling you?"

I carefully weighed the question. God was saying so much and I wanted to make sure I was giving the information He wanted me to.

Finally, I answered, "We are headed for severe judgment in this country."

He seemed shocked. Why would we be heading for judgment? Why would God bring judgment on us?

Now it was my turn to be shocked. This man and his wife were very intelligent. They went to church and attended at least one small group.

Then it really hit me. I believe God ordered this conversation so that I would have a greater understanding of the need for pastors all over this land to receive a word from the Lord about the imminent judgment and disaster that is on the horizon, and the desperate need to repent, both personally and for our nation. Their congregations need to be prepared.

Where, oh where, are the shepherds?
Where are the pastors?
Why are they not
preaching and teaching
truth to their sheep?
Not just a little truth,
but the Bible in its entirety.

Why are they not
preparing their people
for the season
we are living in?
People need to be aware
so they will be ready.

The meeting in Memphis went well, and it was good to spend a little time with our new friends who had issued the invitation. John and I felt this couple would be our dear friends for a long time. We have been so blessed by the people God has connected us with along the way.

After making a number of phone calls, trying in vain to find a place that would look at our generator, we were referred to a place in Conway, Arkansas. It wasn't far, but would take us out of our way a little. I began the saga of leaving messages for someone at this shop, only to have him return my calls and leave a message for me. When he called, my phone didn't even ring, and the message would come through sometime later. I couldn't understand it. Other calls were coming through just fine.

Finally, I sat down and got quiet in order to ask the Lord about it. He was very clear —

> **I didn't tell you to go**
> **to Conway, Arkansas.**
> **I told you to go to Missouri.**

Oh! Well, I would have saved myself a lot of frustration if I would have just asked Him to start with.

> *Isn't that so true*
> *for all of us?*
> *We struggle and strive,*
> *wasting much time and energy.*
> *Only to find*
> *that if we would have*
> *found a quiet place*
> *to be with the Lord,*
> *He would have given us*
> *the answer.*

The morning before we left for Missouri, the Lord woke me up at 1:30am.

> **I have something to tell you,**
> **My child.**

Go on into Missouri.
I have gone before you.
I will open the doors
for who you are to talk to.

Pastors, My child, and others.
But My pastors, My shepherds,
need to hear the message
of the disaster that is coming.

Go. I will take care of you. Go!

Tell of the disaster.

You are the forerunner.
Blowing the trumpet.
Calling out the alarm---
of impending disaster
to this nation.

Go!

We were on the road by 3am, wanting to drive while it was cool. I called my friend, Gina, to let her know when we would be in her area. After hearing about our generator, she offered to call her mechanic to see if he could look at it. Within a few minutes, she had called back to say she had an appointment for the following morning. Now that is God going before you! After all the calls and frustration of not being able to find anyone who could work on our generator, God had worked it out in about ten minutes!

A very pleasant young mechanic fixed our generator the morning we took it in, and for a very reasonable price, too. The icing on the cake was a word from the Lord for that young man. I could tell it touched his heart.

After giving the young man
the word God had given me for him,
I realized he was probably
the reason we hadn't been able
to find anyone

to work on our generator
in all of Memphis.
God had that young mechanic
on His heart
and was setting up
a divine appointment for him.

Gina set up an appointment for us to meet with her pastor. I gave the word from the Lord to him about what is coming to our nation and that he needed to prepare his people. He received it graciously.

I don't know if her pastor changed his message after hearing the word from the Lord or not, but he certainly spoke about what was coming and how the church is asleep.

One comment he made has especially stuck with me.

He said, *"This generation is trying to find the best deck chair on a sinking ship."*

Think about it. How true that is.

The next morning, I went out to fill the car up with gas. Not being familiar with the area, I had intended to get off at the closest exit, but felt strongly that God was leading me to continue on down the road. Two exits later, I knew I was supposed to get off. There was a gas station with better prices right in front of me. That was great...but I still felt there might be more waiting for me at this exit.

As I was pumping gas, a big truck pulled up on the other side of the gas pumps. I didn't pay much attention to it except to think it was really loud.

Then the man spoke to me, "Well, young lady, you're an awful long way from home, aren't you?" At my questioning look, he went on, "I saw your tag. North Carolina. Are you visiting or did you move?"

Some people would have thought he wanted way too much information for a strange man at the gas pumps, but I saw another God set-up.

I began to tell him what my husband and I were doing and that God had given me a message for pastors especially. He pointed to his t-shirt which had an emblem for a Baptist church on it. I smiled and gave him the thumbs up.

He looked me right in the eyes and said, "I'm the pastor. And I believe I was supposed to get gas here today."

I straightened up after tightening my gas cap and gave him the word from the Lord.

> **There is a huge disaster coming to this nation.**
> **You need to prepare your people.**
> **If you do not prepare them,**
> **you will be held accountable.**

He looked at me carefully and then told me he believed that.

We talked a few more minutes and went our separate ways. As I got back on the highway, I realized that I never cease to be amazed at how God sets things up. So often, He just drops them in front of me. Thank You, Lord!

We spoke with two more pastors while we were in Missouri. They were both in churches, but nonetheless God appointments.

Let the wicked forsake his way
And the unrighteous man his thoughts;
And let him return to the Lord,
And He will have compassion on him,
And to our God,
For He will abundantly pardon.

Isaiah 55:7 (NASB)

"What Would He See Today?"

I woke up early Sunday morning, on May 25th. Immediately I heard —

What would he see today?

A scripture came to my mind as I got up to pray. I was familiar with the words, but couldn't put my finger on the reference. I thought it was in Ezekiel and found it very quickly. I will share a few verses with you.

> [5]THEN THE LORD SAID TO ME, "SON OF MAN, LOOK TOWARD THE NORTH." SO I LOOKED, AND THERE TO THE NORTH, BESIDE THE ENTRANCE TO THE GATE OF THE ALTAR, STOOD THE IDOL THAT HAD MADE THE LORD SO ANGRY.
> [6]"SON OF MAN," HE SAID, "DO YOU SEE WHAT THEY ARE DOING? DO YOU SEE THE GREAT SINS THE PEOPLE OF ISRAEL ARE DOING TO DRIVE ME FROM MY TEMPLE? BUT COME, AND YOU WILL SEE EVEN GREATER SINS THAN THESE!"
> [7]THEN HE BROUGHT ME TO THE DOOR OF THE TEMPLE COURTYARD, WHERE I COULD SEE AN OPENING IN THE WALL.
> [8]HE SAID TO ME, "NOW, SON OF MAN, DIG INTO THE WALL." SO I DUG INTO THE WALL AND UNCOVERED A DOOR TO A HIDDEN ROOM.
> [9]"GO IN," HE SAID, "AND SEE THE UNSPEAKABLE WICKEDNESS GOING ON IN THERE!"

¹⁰SO I WENT IN AND SAW THE WALLS ENGRAVED WITH ALL KINDS OF SNAKES, LIZARDS, AND HIDEOUS CREATURES. I ALSO SAW THE VARIOUS IDOLS WORSHIPED BY THE PEOPLE OF ISRAEL. ¹¹SEVENTY LEADERS OF ISRAEL WERE STANDING THERE...EACH OF THEM HELD AN INCENSE BURNER, SO THERE WAS A THICK CLOUD OF INCENSE ABOVE THEIR HEADS. ¹²THEN THE LORD SAID TO ME, "SON OF MAN, HAVE YOU SEEN WHAT THE LEADERS OF ISRAEL ARE DOING WITH THEIR IDOLS IN DARK ROOMS? THEY ARE SAYING, 'THE LORD DOESN'T SEE US; HE HAS DESERTED OUR LAND!'" ¹³THE HE ADDED, "COME, AND I WILL SHOW YOU GREATER SINS THAN THESE!" ¹⁴HE BROUGHT ME TO THE NORTH GATE OF THE LORD'S TEMPLE, AND SOME WOMEN WERE SITTING THERE, WEEPING FOR THE GOD TAMMUZ. ¹⁵"HAVE YOU SEEN THIS?" HE ASKED. "BUT I WILL SHOW YOU EVEN GREATER SINS THAN THESE!" ¹⁶THEN HE BROUGHT ME INTO THE INNER COURTYARD OF THE LORD'S TEMPLE. AT THE ENTRANCE, BETWEEN THE FOYER AND THE BRONZE ALTAR, ABOUT 25 MEN WERE STANDING WITH THEIR BACKS TO THE LORD'S TEMPLE. THEY WERE FACING EASTWARD, WORSHIPING THE SUN! ¹⁷"HAVE YOU SEEN THIS, SON OF MAN?" HE ASKED. "IS IT NOTHING TO THE PEOPLE OF JUDAH THAT THEY COMMIT THESE TERRIBLE SINS, LEADING THE WHOLE NATION INTO VIOLENCE, THUMBING THEIR NOSES AT ME, AND ROUSING MY FURY AGAINST THEM? ¹⁸THEREFORE, I WILL DEAL WITH THEM IN FURY. I WILL NEITHER PITY NOR SPARE THEM. AND THOUGH THEY SCREAM FOR MERCY, I WILL NOT LISTEN."

EZEKIEL 8:5-18 (NLT)

The Lord transported Ezekiel supernaturally to Jerusalem to show him the sinful abominations of the leaders and others. I believe God wanted Ezekiel to see why He would judge them.

As I prayed, I understood clearly what God was telling me. If Ezekiel were to look into the inner chambers, the hidden rooms, of Washington, DC, he would see horrendous abominations being committed.

Think about it, people!
Are we really in any position
to expect God not to judge our nation?

We can repent.
We must repent!
And we should cry out for mercy
to a loving God.

But this country is too far gone
not to realize
God must bring judgment
if we are ever to see true repentance,
and turning back to God.

Two days later I met with a group of very special ladies in the Chicago area. I wasn't sure what I would share with them. Any time I speak, there is so much to share that I could talk for hours. I must be careful to use the time I have wisely, in order to speak the things God would have me to at each and every meeting.

Every lady at that meeting seemed to sense things were different than they had been when we met on previous occasions. I'm not even sure if I can explain what the difference was, and I doubt any of those ladies could either.

At the very end, the lady sitting to my left at the table, turned to me and said, "Maxie, do you think this is the last time I will see you?"

She had tears in her eyes. That very thing had been hanging on the fringes the entire time I had been there. I hadn't felt any liberty to voice it. But now it had been said, quietly, just between the two of us, and I knew it had been on her heart all morning as well.

All I could do was hug her and say, "I don't know. Possibly God will grant us more time together."

Jesus replied,
"If anyone loves me,
he will obey my teaching.
My Father will love him,
and we will come to him
and make our home with him.

John 14:23 (NIV)

The Messenger

There was a pastor of a church in southern Illinois that kept coming to my mind. As I prayed, God gave me a word for that pastor.

> You must stay on the path
> I have chosen for you, My son.
>
> Do not allow yourself to be
> distracted with what others
> want you to do.
> Follow the path I have chosen
> for you.
> Great things await you
> on that path.
>
> This nation is headed for
> the edge of the cliff,
> but you will hold many back.
> You will protect them.
>
> Stay on the path, My son.
> You know what it is.
> You know what it is.
> Stick to it!

I then had a vision of this pastor standing with his back to the edge of the cliff. He had his arms straight out at the sides and, as people rushed toward that edge, his arms stopped them from going over. It seemed they were running, rushing headlong, as though they didn't even realize the cliff was there. When they ran right into his outstretched arms, some fell backwards on the ground, and shook their heads as though they were trying to figure out what had just happened.

This pastor rearranged his day in order to take time to see me. I was able to give the word from the Lord to him and also share the vision God had given me. He was very humble as he listened. Then he shared some things with me.

John and I visited with some friends in the area. God gave us words of encouragement for them and we shared a special time together. All too soon it was time to go.

It wasn't long before we were back in Hickory, North Carolina. We met with a number of people. It was good to be able to share with old friends and new ones as well.

One night while we were in Hickory, I was having a rough night. I just couldn't sleep. Usually I sleep soundly, until God wakes me. Then after praying, reading my Bible, and writing in my journal for a while, I go back to bed and right back to sleep. But this night I felt troubled. Finally, I just got up and God and I had quite a talk. Most of it was personal, and then it changed. This is what God said.

> **For now, My child,**
> **this is what you must say.**
>
> **I have warned.**
> **I have cried out.**
> **I have sent My messengers –**
> **To and fro,**
> **North to South,**
> **East to West.**
>
> **But to no avail.**

To no avail.

The smallest of remnants
has listened and some of those
have dropped by the wayside.

I am sending you out
with a cry for people to
Get Ready! Get Ready!

There will be a remnant,
a small remnant who remains.

There will be places of refuge.
Only a few.

There were more, but many
have turned away and allowed
sin in the camp,
so I will not use them.

Those places will be green
in an otherwise dry land.

But they must not think
too highly of themselves
or I will strike them down.

A short time later the Lord began to speak again.

Do not be deceived!
Do not be deceived, My prophets,
into speaking what they want to hear.

Speak only what I give you.

Stay close to Me.
Spend time with Me.
And you will hear
My words clearly.

**Do not be swayed by others.
Even the prophets leading the land.
Many of those are hearing
only what they want to hear.**

**You *must* speak truth!
No matter how hard it is.**

You must speak truth!

Friends, I wish I could truly convey how I feel when the Lord tells me these things. And I have chosen only a handful, a small handful, of the words He has given me, to share in this book.

In my first book, *From Our Wicked Ways*, I talk about God giving me Ezekiel 33, and the "blood on my hands." Maybe if you read that chapter, you will have a better understanding of how I feel.

*Some of you may say,
"Why do we need
to understand how you feel?"*

*Because possibly,
if more could understand
how I feel,
then more could understand
the call, the burden, the urgency.
And more would get on board
before the people of God
allow this ship to sink.*

Back in Familiar Territory

People had been asking us to come back to South Carolina again. John and I were blessed to be in the Midlands often. It had been a few months since we were there, and after praying about it, we felt the Lord telling us to go.

Just a few days before we arrived in Columbia, the Lord gave me a beautiful word. It is for everyone who wants more of God. I want to share that word with you.

> The heavens are going to break
> forth with rain.
> My rain.
> It will be a cleansing rain,
> a purifying rain.
> It will equip and prepare
> those who need strengthened
> for the days ahead.
>
> It will fall everywhere.
> Absolutely everywhere.
> People must only be open
> to receive it.
>
> Look to the heavens
> with arms open wide
> and breathe in my rain.
>
> It will strengthen you,
> free you, and prepare you
> for what you must walk through
> in the days to come.
> And these days will be soon.
> Do not be deceived.

What a beautiful word!
I can just picture us,
all of us who are longing
for more of God,
standing outside
with our arms open wide,
and our faces turned to the sky...
Soaking up
that soft, sweet, exhilarating rain
of the Holy Spirit.

There were a number of meetings scheduled in the Columbia area. They would be held at different venues and there would be a variety of people from different denominations in each group. I would be speaking on Sunday morning, Wednesday night, at an intercessory prayer meeting, a ladies meeting, and a luncheon meeting.

God began to talk to me about those meetings and what He would have me to say.

1. **The first and most important thing is to make sure you are saved.** Do you have a relationship with Jesus?

2. **Is your heart right with God?** Have you wandered away from Him? Do you need to restore your relationship with the Lord?

3. **Reach the Lost.** The time is short and we are living in a season of much uncertainty. We need to reach as many people with the gospel as possible.

4. **Learn to hear God's voice clearly.** Spend time with Him, listening to what He wants to tell you.

5. **Spend time in His word.** Make sure you read your Bible every day.

6. **Repent.** Keep a short record with God. Make sure your heart is clear of any wrongdoing. Have you done anything that isn't pleasing to God? Possibly even your thoughts or attitude hasn't been what it should be. Ask Him to forgive you and keep your heart clean.

7. **Prepare.** Whatever God has put on your heart, do it! Don't delay! We all need to have enough food, water, and necessities to last our family for a few weeks. That is simply wisdom. God is speaking to some to stock up supplies like a storehouse. To others He is telling them to store up Bibles and blankets. We need to know what our job is and be obedient to do it.

8. **Stand.** We need to make a decision in our hearts that we will stand for Jesus – no matter what! If you aren't certain you can do that, get alone with the Lord and pray. Pray until you feel you are strong enough that you won't deny Christ under any circumstance.

I understand you would all rather hear that revival is coming, and I would much rather carry a message of revival. We will see an awakening in this country. However, I believe we are going to experience some very difficult times of judgment before that awakening happens.

Even though God has given me a hard message, we need to understand this is an exciting time we are living in. We are going to see God do the most amazing miracles! He is going to protect us and provide for us in supernatural ways. But we must draw near to Him, spend time with Him, and learn to trust Him unconditionally.

When you have a problem, go to God first. If you are struggling with something, get alone with the Lord. You may still need to see a doctor or do something in the natural to help with your problem, but give God a chance to take care of it. You may just receive a miracle!

It was time to leave Columbia. I had mixed feelings, as always, when leaving this area. It was hard to leave all these dear people, people who loved on us and treated us with such reverence. But while I hated to leave, I knew God had things for us to do, and we felt the urgency of getting on the road.

"But you, when you pray, go into your inner room,
close your door and pray
to your Father who is in secret,
and your Father who sees
what is done in secret
will reward you."

Matthew 6:6 (NASB)

Minnesota, North Dakota, South Dakota

These three states had been coming to my mind more and more frequently for about a month. This is one way God often speaks to me. Something will continually come to my mind, and I will begin to pray about it. Then, usually in the middle of the night, God will speak clearly to me about what we are to do. That's what happened this time. We knew it would be early September when we headed north, so after a stop in Hickory at our storage unit to switch out our summer things for fall and winter, we once again drove to our daughter's in Knoxville.

We have been so thankful to have a free and comfortable place to park between trips. Their driveway accommodates the motor home nicely and what's more important is how our daughter and son-in-law welcome us with open arms every time we need to stop there. (Not to mention we get to be with those grandbabies!)

As we were preparing for this trip, John found a motor home in the paper. They were asking $30,000. We sure didn't have that kind of money, but it was just a few miles away so we went to check it out. God had been speaking to me about a new motor home for a few months. Nothing specific; however, I knew that God was aware of our need for a newer model that was in better shape. Our motor home had served us well for almost three years, and it was still fine for going to the campground a few times a year, but we were extremely vulnerable being on the road as much as we were, and we lived in that motor home. It needed to be in good shape. So we decided to go look at this one.

What a disappointment. It was so dirty and smelled awful. Getting out of there as quickly as possible, we went back home.

As we walked up the steps and into our home, John and I both said, "Thank You, Lord, for what You have given us." It was clean, smelled nice, and we were both so thankful for what we had.

The following morning, John was out in the driveway checking the outside compartments to make sure we had what we needed to hit the road. A neighbor from down the street drove by. She felt like she needed to back up and talk to John. John had spent some time with her husband when we first got this motor home. They had owned RVs for years and he was able to give John a lot of good advice and offered his help whenever we needed it. Her husband had passed away about a year earlier. As the lady was talking with John, she told him she was selling their coach and we should come down and look at it. He said he would tell me and thanked her.

I had seen their coach a time or two. They kept it inside a building most of the time, but when it was in their driveway, you couldn't help but notice it. My first thought was there is no way we can afford that! And I told John so. But we went down to look at it since the lady had invited us.

It was even more impressive inside than out. It looked brand new and smelled like new leather. We were shocked when she told us she would love to have it used for the Lord and would sell it to us for $30,000 if we wanted it. Wow! After telling her we would pray about it and get back to her, we walked back to Michael and Candi's. They began to encourage us right away, offering to help with fundraising and getting the word out.

The Lord was very clear in letting us know we should move forward on this. John and I were in total agreement about what He was telling us.

We went back to talk to the owner, asking if we could put down $1000 and if she would give us time to raise the money. She was kind enough to tell us she would do that, but wanted to know how much time we were talking about.

"Thirty days," I said.

She seemed surprised, but not nearly as surprised as I was. I hadn't even thought about a time frame. But obviously God had.

> *That night I was up praying,*
> *really talking to the Lord*
> *about how quickly this was happening*
> *and how overwhelming it was.*
> *God spoke to me about a particular lady.*
> *He told me she would*
> *"finish it off."*
> *I wasn't sure what He meant by that*
> *and didn't feel like I should*
> *question Him about it.*
> *I told John about what the Lord*
> *had said to me*
> *and wrote it in my journal.*
> *I didn't ever forget it,*
> *but I didn't talk about it anymore.*
> *I suppose you could say*
> *I just hid it in my heart.*

We got busy sending out support letters to our faithful friends. Michael and Candi were busy as well, doing all they could do to let people know and to help raise the funds needed to make that motor home a reality for us. But without a doubt, the most important thing they did was to encourage us. Their encouragement was absolutely vital during this time and never once did either of them let us down.

Minnesota, North Dakota, and South Dakota were still waiting, and soon it was time for us to head north. We would have to leave the fundraising in God's hands.

I have really enjoyed looking at maps for as long as I can remember. I can read and look over an atlas for hours. The trip was planned out and we were ready to go. Then God began to change things a little. He was telling me we needed to go through Illinois. That wasn't the most direct route and, so as to not drive more miles than necessary, I hadn't included Illinois in the trip. As we got on the highway though, I knew I would have to make some changes. My family was in Illinois and it would be good to see my aunt again. I didn't think that was the purpose for God rerouting our plans, but we would leave the "whys" up to Him and just be obedient.

We spent a few days with family and had a great time. The time I spent with my aunt was extremely special. We talked and prayed and sang songs together about Jesus and heaven. She was 92 years young and, although her voice was soft, she could still harmonize beautifully. That nursing home room was transformed by those songs. Residents and staff alike would pause outside the open door to listen as we sang.

My Nankie (as I had called her all my life) was more like a mother to me than an aunt. She was in very poor health, but didn't complain. She always had a smile for me and wanted to hold my hand the entire time I was there.

As I prayed for her and kissed her for the last time before we left, I was so thankful to the Lord for giving me this special time with her.

A Bar in Iowa

Soon it was time to continue on our trip. God had another surprise in store for John and I. One we hadn't even considered. Once again, we had intended to stay on the interstates, taking the most direct route into Minnesota. Near Cedar Falls, God directed us to get onto a two-lane road and go north. As I began to search the map, I realized He was taking us directly through Nashua, Iowa. This probably doesn't mean a whole lot to most of you, but to John and I, it was quite a gift. You see, we had gotten married at The Little Brown Church in the Vale in Nashua almost twenty-five years ago. We had never made a trip back to that little church and, honestly, I had been too focused on where God was sending us, and the message God had, to even think about Nashua, Iowa.

As soon as we drove into town, God told us to stop at the Welcome Center. We went in, looked around, and talked to the lady at the desk. The Holy Spirit was whispering in my ear that we were to take Bibles inside. After getting a stack of Bibles out of the motor home and praying over them, we went back into the Welcome Center. We weren't even sure if they would let us leave them, but God had spoken, so we knew He had a plan. Sure enough, the lady was thrilled to get the Bibles. She said they would be kept on her counter, free to anyone who wanted one.

Walking back to the motor home, hand in hand, we smiled. It thrills our hearts to see God work and know He allowed us to have a small part in it.

As we drove on, I saw a small green sign that read "Business District." The Holy Spirit was telling me we should turn there. By the time I told John, he had passed the street, but he made a U-turn and went back.

It was a small downtown area with those diagonal parking places in front of the stores. There weren't many cars around, so we didn't feel bad taking up a lot of parking spaces with our motor home towing the car.

I had no idea what I was supposed to do here. Directly across the street, a church occupied two or three storefronts. Since God sends me to a lot of churches and pastors, we went there first. There were people inside, but the doors were all locked. It was Saturday afternoon.

We went back to the motor home. I wasn't going to just guess at what God wanted me to do and I had no direction at the moment, so we would go back inside to pray.

Just as we stepped inside, I looked out the big window straight across the street again. There was another sign I hadn't paid much attention to when we first pulled up. "Hometown Bar." The sign really stood out to me now. And I heard the Lord speak to me.

You need to preach in there.

My heart was pounding. I could feel the presence of the Holy Spirit.

"John, I need to preach in that bar."

He said, "You mean, you need to go in that bar."

"No. I need to preach in that bar."

I heard a sigh and then, "Well, let's go in the bar then."

As we walked in, I blinked as my eyes were adjusting to how dim it was in there. There were only a few people sitting up at the bar. A lady bartender spoke to us.

God gave us the opening right away.

"Is there a grocery store anywhere around?" I asked.

"Nope. Not anymore," a customer replied.

Another man started talking to John. He asked John if he knew where such and such road was and John told him we weren't from around there.

"Where are you from?" The bartender asked. And that was the open door. We began to talk about traveling across the country calling America back to God. She said, "Oh! We sure need that!"

And I was off! Like God had shot me out of a cannon. Standing in the middle of the floor preaching. I have no idea what I even said, all I know is that I had everybody's attention and John was staring at me. He is used to a lot of strange things with this wife of his, but this even shocked him.

I do know it was not a condemning message, and I preached for about fifteen minutes. I really don't know much else about what I said. I believe God was just speaking through me.

Near the end I said, "Can I get an Amen?"

At that point John's mouth fell open! He has probably never heard me say that in all the times he has listened to me speak. That just isn't a phrase I use.

But it must have struck a chord because the bartender hit the bar a couple of times and said, "Yes! Yes!"

I walked over to stand in front of her. I knew she was the reason God had sent me in here. Who knows how many times He had tried to get her to go to church, so He decided to bring church to her.

She started talking to me. "You know, everybody I meet is depressed. They have lost their jobs, their homes, and some have even lost their families. No one has any hope. They have just about given up."

She really looked at me. I was quiet because I knew she had more to say. Then she continued, "But you. You come in here smiling, laughing, like you're on top of the world. And even though you know this country is going to hell in a hand basket, you have hope. And I know God sent you in here because I needed to hear all that. Thank you so much."

John went out to get a copy of my book for her. I wrote her name in the front cover, along with a message for her, and signed it.

She reached out to take hold of my hand for a moment. I told her to make sure she was right with God. She smiled, thanked me again, and said she would do that.

John and I walked out of the Hometown Bar as though we were walking on air. Bless that bartender, Lord. Let her never forget this day.

A few miles down the road we pulled into a gravel area under some big trees right next to the little church where our wedding had been. The lady in the shop gave us permission to park there overnight. The following morning, we attended that church and had lunch with them afterward. I gave the pastor a copy of my book.

As we got back on the road
I opened my Bible
and saw a bookmark
given to me by
my Chinese friend.

"Enlarge your tent curtains wide.
Do not hold back,

lengthen your cords,
strengthen your stakes.
Isaiah 54:2"

God, what are You showing me?

We continued on and after a few days felt led to stop in a town a little south of Minneapolis. The first night we were there I was up with the Lord and He gave me a word for pastors.

> **Tell them this country is under**
> **judgment and severe persecution**
> **is coming.**
>
> **Tell them they need to make certain**
> **they can stand when the time comes-**
> **and it will come - especially for pastors.**
>
> **They need not fear to take a stand**
> **for Me because I will take care of**
> **My own.**
>
> **These pastors have been hand-picked,**
> **chosen by Me, for such a time as this.**
> **I will provide all they need**
> **to do what I have called them to do.**
> **But they must do it My way.**
> **Relinquish the reins to Me.**
> **And I will guide them every step**
> **of the way.**
>
> **It's coming quickly.**
> **It's coming fast.**
> **Be ready.**
>
> **Do not be caught with your hands**
> **on the reins.**
> **Allow Me to do the leading.**

I spoke with two pastors there. One was a lady pastor of a big Baptist church in the downtown area. She was so gracious to me.

She seemed almost humbled that God would send a messenger to her. We talked for quite a while and then prayed together.

It was interesting how we were led to the other pastor. John was driving around a block and I just couldn't seem to get a release to leave that area. I don't know how many times we circled that block.

Finally, as John looked up ahead he said, "Look up there. I think we've located the reason you felt we had to stay in this area."

I looked up to see a Catholic priest out walking his dog. We had to laugh, wondering how long that dog had been trying to get his master to take him for a walk.

I got out to speak with the priest. I may have scared him initially, but he relaxed as we talked. I gave the word from the Lord to him and a copy of my book.

Later that night, I received a phone call from a pastor friend of ours. When he found out where we were, he wanted us to meet some friends of his. I told him we had planned to leave the next morning, but would try to wait long enough to meet his friends.

I told the Lord we really needed them to call us early if we were going to be able to meet them. We received the call around eight in the morning and arranged to meet this couple for dinner.

We must have talked for three or four hours. They wanted to hear everything. We had such a blessed time together and all too soon it was time to go.

We drove a short distance and stopped at another Walmart. The next morning, we would drive into North Dakota.

The Dakotas

As we came into North Dakota, the Holy Spirit began to speak to me about parking at a church instead of a Walmart parking lot.

We stopped to park the motor home and unhook the car so we could drive to a church God had shown us. The pastor was kind and welcoming. The only thing he asked us to do was to pray over the ground where they were getting ready to build, sometime while we were there. We thanked him and left to get the motor home.

We spent three days in that church parking lot. God led us to some interesting people. One of those days, as we were driving, I felt we should stop at a yard sale. There were signs for yard sales all over, but there was only one I sensed we were supposed to stop at.

As we looked around at things on the tables, I was waiting to see what God had brought us there for. Three senior citizens were sitting at the table taking money. They started talking about the state our country was in. I walked a little closer and listened. They were all three really disturbed about things that were taking place and the direction our country was heading.

John had been listening, too, and we walked over to the table to talk with them. We told them we were traveling across the country calling America back to God. John told them that God is the answer to our troubles, not politics. We had their attention and God took advantage of it. He continued to give us words to encourage them. When we said our good-byes, we all knew God had brought us together.

It would be impossible to share even half of the meetings and encounters we have had on this journey. I'm thankful I am not the one who has to make the decisions about which stories go in the book and which ones will be left out. Sometimes I try to leave something out and God simply will not let me get very far ahead before I go back and write about it. Other times I put things in that I have to go back and delete. God is running this show and I am very happy to leave Him in charge.

There is one more story from North Dakota that I know must be included. It occurred the morning we were leaving.

265

John had already hooked up the car and had everything ready to get on the road. He came back inside to find me sitting on the bed looking like I had every intention of being there awhile. I was trying to locate something on my phone. When John questioned what that might be, I told him I was looking for an address for the mayor's office.

He looked at me for a minute and then said very calmly, "Sweetie, we can't take this motor home through downtown. That's probably where you would find the mayor. And I have already hooked up the car. Do I need to unhook it?" (Sometimes I think this husband of mine may be approaching sainthood and other times...)

"No, no, don't unhook it. Just give me a minute."

He didn't look convinced, but went toward the front to make another cup of coffee.

I found a phone number for a mayor's office, but after I made the call and spoke with a lady I knew it wasn't the person I needed to connect with.

I stopped looking and started praying.

About that time John came back and said, "I think you are trying to call the wrong mayor. I believe the Lord is saying you need to call the mayor from another city." He then named the city.

Wow! As soon as he said that I knew he was right on target. I looked for a number to the mayor's office for the city John had mentioned. It was easily located. A man answered and I knew it was the mayor I was looking for. The number was his personal cell phone.

After introducing myself, I briefly told him about our ministry. Then told him I had a word from the Lord for him and asked if it would be all right if I gave it to him over the phone. I let him know I would have preferred to give it to him in person, but that wasn't going to be possible this time.

He was silent for a moment and then said, "This is very unusual, but yes, that would be fine."

This is the word God gave me for that mayor.

> **You will need to make a very important decision in the upcoming days.**
>
> **Be sure you make it on the side of the Lord.**

He began to talk to me. About decisions he had made over this past year and decisions coming up. Then he told me he used to go to church and be closer to God, but life got in the way. Now he found himself so busy that he didn't have time for church. He said he probably needed to start going again.

Then he told me he talks to God. He said some people would say he was talking to himself, but, "I know better," he said. "And I believe God hears me."

I told him I was sure God heard him. I thanked him for his time and for listening before we hung up.

I got up from the bed and told John I was ready to go. He just smiled and got behind the wheel.

A few hours later we were in South Dakota. I grabbed a napkin off the dash and started scribbling on it. John knew I had heard something from the Lord.

> **They must be stopped at the gate.**
> **Once they get in, it will be too late.**

That was it. I had no idea what it meant, but knew God would let me know when I needed to.

We found a great Walmart parking lot to stop in. They had an area for RVs to park, out of the way of other vehicles, with trees for shade. It was very nice.

The next day was Saturday and we prayed as we drove around a bit. God didn't let us down. He showed us the church we were to attend the next morning.

John gave the pastor a prayer card and a copy of my book. The message was good and we enjoyed being there. We headed south that afternoon.

As we were going down the road, I opened my Bible and took out the church bulletin from that morning. My mouth dropped open. How could I not have seen it? I couldn't believe I missed that connection. God must have hidden it from me until now for some reason.

Right on the front of that bulletin and on a bookmark and a card inside was the name of the church. *The Church at the Gate.* I still couldn't believe I hadn't noticed it during church.

That night I prayed about the word God had given me about "at the gate." Should I have given that word to the pastor?

The next day I had an email from him. He told me he had a reading list a mile long and seldom has time to read a book. However, he had felt compelled to read my book and couldn't put it down until he had finished it. He felt what I was hearing was from the Lord and wanted to thank me for the book. He invited us to stop in again anytime we were in the area. I emailed him back with the word from the Lord and when God had given it to me. God had made the connection exactly as He wanted it done.

The Road Gets Rocky

We had no idea when we left that church what the next forty-eight hours would hold. We would experience three breakdowns in the motor home and my dear sweet aunt would go home to be with the Lord.

The first breakdown was Sunday evening. John knew something was wrong with the motor home. It was almost dark and we had to find a place to stop. Then we saw a McDonald's with a big sign advertising they had truck parking. Thank You, Lord. We could get off the road at a safe place until morning.

It was very dusty with all the trucks pulling in and out, but it was well lit and there was a McDonald's within walking distance. Not much else, but it could be worse.

We slept a little that night and in the morning called our roadside assistance. While waiting for a mechanic to come, I felt led to walk over to McDonald's. I sat in there looking around, just waiting to see what I was actually supposed to be doing in there.

A couple came in and stood looking at the menu. The man then came and sat down at a table near where I was sitting. The lady came over to him shortly and asked if he had any change at all. He said he didn't.

She went back to the counter and I knew why God had sent me in there. I went to the counter and heard her ordering one hamburger and one coffee, obviously for them to share. I told her to order what she wanted and then told the cashier I would be right back with the money. I ran back to the motor home, grabbed a twenty-dollar bill and took it back.

The lady had stepped away from the counter and hadn't finished ordering. I gave her the money and told her to get what she wanted. She pushed the money back to me. I told her I was a Chaplain, my husband and I were in full-time ministry, and we had broken down and were waiting for a mechanic. Then she really didn't want to take the money, saying she was sure we needed it for the ministry. Finally, I told her God had sent me in there specifically for her and her husband and that He wanted me to buy their lunch. It was really from God, not from me. With tears in her eyes, she accepted the money and told me thank you.

She asked if I would sit with them when she came back with their food. So I did. What a precious couple. He was a diesel mechanic and had lost his job and then their home. Unable to find another job, they were driving to stay with their daughter for a while.

All they owned was packed in their car. But they were still smiling and so thankful God had sent me to them. The man offered to look at the motor home if I wanted him to, but by that time the mechanic had arrived. I was so thankful to have met them and to be used by the Lord to be a part of making their day a little better.

The mechanic determined it was the alternator belt. It took a couple of hours for him to get one and bring it back. After putting it on, the motor home started, but the battery wasn't charging like John thought it should. The mechanic insisted it would charge more when we got on the road.

Meanwhile, we had been talking to the young mechanic about Jesus. We asked if we could pray for him and if he would like a Bible. He seemed grateful for both.

We paid the bill and got back on the road.

We got about twenty miles before we began to have major problems again. The motor home was backfiring and the battery power was dropping dangerously low. We got off at an exit and called the roadside assistance again.

While we sat in the motor home, waiting for the mechanic to come, I got a phone call. My sweet aunt had gone to be with Jesus. It was a promotion for her and I was thankful she was no longer suffering, but my heart was breaking. I simply couldn't imagine life without her. She had been the stabilizing influence in my life as I was growing up and was the only person that I felt loved me unconditionally for many years. Honestly, I'm not even sure if I would be alive today had it not been for my Nankie. I had always felt like she was my angel in human form that God had sent to love and protect me. And now she was gone.

They sent out the same young mechanic. He didn't look at the work he had done earlier, just said we would have to have a new battery. Another $200, and we were back on the road. For about forty miles.

The new battery was dropping dangerously low and the backfiring was horrible. It was close to midnight and nowhere to stop. Every time we got to the top of a huge hill, we would see another one up ahead.

John would say, "There is no way we will make it to the top of that one."

And I would say, "God is going to get us to the exact place we need to be!"

Over and over again I proclaimed that. We could see a sign for Love's Travel Center down the road and, as we got closer, there was a smaller sign that read "Mechanic on duty 24 hours." Thank You, Lord!

We drove into the station, all the way around to the back, and pulled right up in front of the open door to the service bay. A mechanic came out to see what we needed and the engine died. Exactly where we needed to be! Exactly. Not one foot less. It took those mechanics about five minutes to find the problem. The first mechanic had tightened the alternator belt too tight and it was now in shreds. The automotive parts store down the street would be open for only fifteen more minutes. But the belt was so shredded they couldn't find the number needed to get a replacement.

I started praying and within about one minute one of the mechanics said, "I don't believe this!" as he held up one small strip of that belt with the entire number on it.

I smiled at him and said, "I prayed."

He said, "You must have. There's no way this could happen with how messed up this belt is. Most of it isn't even here anymore. You lost pieces of it on the road."

One of the guys went to get the new belt and they had it on in about thirty minutes. They charged us almost nothing and wrote on our receipt what the first mechanic had done in case we wanted to try to get our money back. Those guys even offered us a place to park for the night if we wanted to stay there since it was so late. God certainly got us to the exact place we needed to be.

John and I prayed about
contacting that shop
to get our money back
because of the mistake
the first mechanic had made.

We couldn't get any peace
about doing that and
felt we should just leave it alone.
No amount of money
was worth the witnessing
that had taken place
with that young mechanic.
We didn't want him to lose his job
or get in trouble at work
and have that horrible memory
every time he looked at his Bible
we had given him.
Or any Bible for that matter.
So we just left it
in the Lord's most capable hands.

The next morning, we continued on our way to Lawrenceburg, Tennessee, where my aunt's funeral would be. It was only a few miles out of our way since we were headed for Knoxville anyway. Once again, I thanked the Lord for putting us where we needed to be. We were close enough to be able to attend her funeral and I was so grateful for that.

So often we struggle
with things
trying to work them out
on our own.
Or we are so determined
to make sure we get
what's coming to us,
that we fight battles

we were never intended to fight.

In Exodus 14:14, we read,
"The Lord shall fight for you,
and ye shall hold your peace."

John and I have encountered
a number of people
who hear the story
and think we should have
complained about the mechanic.

I'm not saying a person
should never complain or report
a bad situation.
But we need to be very cautious
when stepping out to fight a battle,
that it is indeed a battle
we were intended to fight.

The Lord is much more capable
of fighting our battles
than we are.
And if we leave those battles
in His hands,
we never have to be concerned
with the outcome.

"Bring the whole tithe into the storehouse,
So that there may be food in My house,
And test me now in this," says the Lord of hosts,
"if I will not open for you the windows of heaven
and pour out for you a blessing until it overflows."

Malachi 3:10 (NASB)

Promises of the Lord

There had been so much going on for the past week or so we barely had time to even think about the new motor home. We knew donations were coming in, but didn't have a lot of the details. I was awake one night praying, and the Lord told me —

The motor home is yours.
I have told you.
Now rest in it.

And I did.

God was also so gracious in the peace He gave me about the passing of my sweet aunt. I knew there would be many days down the road of wishing I could talk to her, hear her sing those harmony parts, and feel the soft, gentle touch of her hands, but I knew she was singing in heaven. I didn't ever have to wonder where she was. The peace of the Lord, that peace that passes anything we can understand, is a wonderful place to be, and God just kept me in that place.

God had given me words at different times about a new motor home for John and I. Of course, as we all tend to do, I got ahead of Him a few times and thought it would happen sooner than it did.

We arrived back in Knoxville in late September. Donations had continued to roll in, but now they appeared to be at a standstill.

On Wednesday, October 1st, I told John he should call the lady and tell her we would sign the papers in one week, on October 8th. He asked me a logical question.

"How much money do we have for the motor home?"

"$17,000," I replied.

"Okay. I'll call her."

On Friday, the 3rd, Candi helped me put our other motor home on Craigslist. God spoke to me that night and said —

It will sell on Wednesday.

On Sunday, Candi and Michael asked if anyone had inquired about it. I told them no one had, but that God had told me it would sell on Wednesday. They just looked at me and didn't say a word.

On Monday I received an email from a guy who left his phone number. He and I played phone tag Monday and Tuesday and were never able to catch up with each other.

Tuesday night around 11:30, I noticed there was a new email. I contacted him Wednesday morning. He wanted to buy a used RV and needed to do it that very day because of his schedule. He had been looking for one for a while and wanted to know if he and his wife could see ours later that day. They lived a few hours away and we offered to drive a couple of hours toward them so the trip wouldn't be so long.

Our daughter helped us get everything boxed up and out of our motor home. We had been working on it, but it appeared we were down to the wire. Within about two hours we had the motor home cleaned out and ready to go. I had no doubt these people would buy it. After all, God had told me it would sell on Wednesday.

A friend on our ministry team and his wife had offered to loan us $6000 toward purchasing the new one. That was now in the bank.

Then I spoke with a lady on the phone who asked how much we needed? I told her $7000. She called back to say she wanted to "finish it off." I was speechless! Partly because of the generous heart of this precious lady, but also because of the wording she had used. God had told me in the very beginning this lady would "finish it off," and His promises always hold true.

We had exactly enough for the new motor home! It still didn't seem possible that in just a few hours, that beautiful coach would belong to us.

We met the gentleman and his wife so they could look at our motor home. I had followed John in the car so we would have a way to get back. Sure enough, just as God had promised, those people bought our motor home. They paid $6000 cash. Exactly what we needed to pay our friends the amount they had loaned us in case we needed it. In twenty-four hours we had paid them back for the loan. God intended for that new motor home to be free and clear!

There is so much more I could say.
Miraculous details
of how everything fell into place
for this amazing gift God had given us.
From the first donation
of $20,
to the pastor who had
taken donations for
the taxes and registration-
having no idea of how much we needed.
Yet he ended up with
almost the exact dollar amount
on the very day we
needed it.
Lord, we cannot thank You enough.

If you walk in My statutes
and keep My commandments
so as to carry them out,
Then I shall give you
rains in their season,
so that the land
will yield its produce
and the trees of the field
will bear their fruit.

Leviticus 26:3-4 (NASB)

Hearing Is Not Enough

Around the middle of October, 2014, I had a dream that I will never forget.

In this dream, John and I were on a two-lane road in the motor home. It was a beautiful day. We were laughing and talking, enjoying the scenery.

All of a sudden it seemed like God screamed in my right ear!

TURN RIGHT!
RIGHT NOW!

I told John to turn right, right here! There was a little road he was able to slow down enough to get turned into. We had barely made the turn when we both saw a little sign that said "Private Drive."

John looked at me as though to say, "Now what?" Being a smart man, he didn't speak a word. We could see a house just a short distance away and it looked like the lane ended there.

Then we heard the explosion. We looked up to our left through the trees and could see big pieces of something flying up into the air. The bridge! The explosion had taken out the bridge that had been just ahead of us on the road we had turned off of.

That was when I realized God had been speaking to me for miles. I had heard Him...telling me that we needed to turn. *Turn on this road, turn on that road. Turn here, my child. You need to get off this road.*

I knew the voice of the Lord. I had heard him telling me, urging me, to get off the road we were on. It wasn't that I was ignoring Him, but I was looking for the "perfect" road to turn onto. Knowing the difficulties of turning the motor home around and not being able to back up when we are towing the car, I had been looking at roads for a long while, and hadn't seen one I thought was suitable for us to turn on. Realization kicked in. I had heard God telling me what we should do. Over and over again. But in looking for what I thought was the perfect place to turn, we could have lost our lives in that explosion on the bridge.

How many of us do this
on a daily basis?
We hear God,
we know His voice,
But we aren't obedient.
I wasn't consciously
being disobedient.
I was just going down the road,
enjoying the beautiful day,
hearing the Lord,
being totally unaware
of the urgency.

Take care, my friend,
that you are not doing this, too.
It could be your life.

This was a dream. However, it could just as easily have been real life. God, in His grace, got my attention. But we must not fall into a habit of hearing and not being *immediately obedient.* That's a very dangerous road to be on.

And remember...95% obedience
is not obedience.

The Angel on Dauphin Island

The pastor of Dauphin Island United Methodist Church had asked us when we could come back to the island. God had already been speaking to me about going back there. I felt this visit to Dauphin Island would somehow be different from the other times we had been there.

We arrived on October 16 and had intended to stay until around mid-December, but God had other plans. He allowed us to stay just long enough to see what is quite possibly the most amazing vision I have ever experienced, then He was very clear that it was time for us to move on.

As you read of my experience from that night, I hope you will ask the Lord to give you supernatural understanding of this vision.

The window was open beside my bed; it was a warm night on the island. John and I were parked in a different spot than usual. Our new motor home wouldn't fit in the one we had stayed in before, which was on the other side of the campground. My window allowed me to see the street and the bike path. We were directly across from the ferry landing. It was so bright from the floodlights that I could see the area almost as well as if it was day.

As I lay there, trying to figure out what awakened me, I heard something. It was a strange sound. Lying so still, barely breathing, I continued to listen. The sound was getting louder and closer, a wailing almost. I thought someone must be hurt or in need of help.

I believe I saw her and was able to distinguish the words at the same time. She was running down the bike path just outside the fence. Not running, jogging maybe, in what appeared to be slow motion. I don't know if she was literally moving in slow motion, or if that's just how I saw her. Of average height and build, with dark hair, almost black. The thing my eyes fixed on was the veil on her head. It was white, with a thin shiny white ribbon that ran around the edge of the gauzy material. It looked to be one layer of material and streamed out behind her as she ran. It had to be six to eight feet long.

Briefly, I considered what kind of person would be out jogging in the middle of the night dressed like that!

But the voice, the sound of her voice, was what caught my attention even more. It was truly somewhere between a wail and a cry, coming from way down inside her. I've never heard anything like it, before or since.

> *"Repent! Repent! Judgment is at hand!*
> *Repent! Repent!"*

> *"Repent! The Kingdom of God is at hand!*
> *Repent! Repent!"*

She continued to cry out as she jogged in slow motion on past our motor home. I couldn't take my eyes off of her.

I didn't move, just lay there listening to her voice fade as she went on past the campground until her voice faded out and I was unable to hear her.

There was nowhere for her to go in that direction in the middle of the night. The Sea Lab was just past the campground and then

282

there was the old fort. Then the point, where land ended and the ocean began.

It wasn't long before I could hear her voice faintly again. It sounded as if she had turned around and was heading back. She got closer and closer and I was able to hear the words clearly again. Then she just stopped. Seemingly almost as if she was directly behind the motor home. I never saw her again.

I lay still for a little while, then picked up my phone to look at the time. It was shortly after midnight. Those who know me well would attest to the fact that if I cannot tell you the exact time, I had to be rattled.

What on earth had I just witnessed? It didn't even occur to me at the time that she could possibly be an angel. Except for the sound of her voice, which was definitely not of this world, she looked fairly normal. Except for that veil, of course. And the strange way she was jogging in slow motion. I believe she had on black pants and a black top but, to be honest, I can't say for sure.

And the sound of her voice...I do not think I will ever forget what she sounded like.

"Repent! Repent!! Judgment is at hand!"

God help us.

Finally I got up to pray.

> *I suppose there was some expectation*
> *on my part that God would*
> *tell me what I had just*
> *encountered.*
> *But as I prayed...and waited...*
> *He calmed my spirit, but didn't*
> *really tell me anything about the girl.*
>
> *I call her a girl.*
> *Initially, I thought she looked about 20.*
> *But later, I realized she looked*

rather old in a way.
A way I can't really explain.

It was Tuesday, November 11th, 2014, when I saw her. On Wednesday evening, the Lord spoke to me about what I had seen.

When we are on Dauphin Island, John and I always go to the Wednesday night service at the Methodist Church. We feel like we are missing something if we can't make it. It seems as though the people there truly gather together to encourage each other and most importantly to meet God.

But late in the afternoon, I began to feel that I just had to stay home that night. I tried to make myself go and ended up in tears. Finally, John told me he would go but that he thought I should stay home. He knew I needed to be with the Lord.

As soon as John walked out the door, I grabbed my Bible and went to sit on the bed. I opened it to my daily consecutive reading, which happened to be in the book of Isaiah. I had read four chapters that morning and chapter 63 was next. I started to read.

It begins with God's future judgment upon an ungodly world. As I read I asked Him, "God, do You want to tell me something about this?"

This is what He said to me —

> **It's upon us, My child. It's here.**
> **Literally right around the corner.**
> **And no one is paying any attention**
> **except a very small remnant.**
>
> **That vision was a warning.**
> **You aren't the only one who saw**
> **and heard her.**
> **She was heard around the world**
> **by a chosen few.**

It was then I realized I had seen an angel.

I cannot say the Lord specifically told me this,
but I truly felt He had sent that angel out
as sort of a last-ditch effort.
Maybe the very sound of her cry
penetrating the atmosphere
would somehow make a difference.
I don't know.
I only know I have never
forgotten that night.
And I doubt I ever will.

Dauphin Island, Alabama seems to be a special place set aside for spiritual happenings from the Lord. I have had dreams and visions from the Lord since the first night I stayed there, a few years ago.

I cannot say for sure there is a connection here but, in the early 1500's, Mobile Bay was named *The Bay of the Holy Spirit.* Dauphin Island is at the mouth of Mobile Bay. At some point the name was changed to Mobile Bay. However, in God's eyes it may still be *The Bay of the Holy Spirit.*

A few days after seeing the angel, God was very clear it was time for John and I to leave the island. Although not wanting to go, we obediently hit the road.

Shortly thereafter, I woke up very early one morning and knew I needed to get up to pray. Almost immediately, I realized something felt strange. Unable to put my finger on it, I sat quietly before the Lord for a while.

It felt too calm somehow. Usually, when I get up in the night to pray I have such a burden for what is taking place in our nation. Oh, I pray about all sorts of things, whatever the Holy Spirit brings to my mind, but the state of our nation and the mess we are in is never far from my heart. But tonight...something was different.

For almost 20 years, God has been speaking to me about repentance. He has given me words of repentance for individuals; friends, family, and strangers. He has given me words for groups, churches, and pastors, many of those messages having to do with repentance. Twenty years is a long time to walk in that place with the Lord and, now this morning, it almost felt as if that burden was gone. I wasn't at all sure what to make of that.

Over the next 24 hours it kind of settled on me. God was no longer calling our nation to repentance. And that could only mean one thing. *Judgment is near!*

As a nation we certainly have not turned back to God. If anything, we are doing just the opposite. It almost seems to me as if our country is trying it's hardest to get farther and farther away from God at a breathtaking speed. Moral values are definitely a thing of the past. Today, if one speaks up about moral Godly values, it is labeled as hate speech.

No. The United States has not turned back to God. God has not decided our behavior is okay, or to look the other way while we make fools of ourselves.

I am speaking to the people of God here!

The world cannot be expected to live Godly lives. But as Christians, we have a mandate to act Christ-like. As a whole we have fallen far short of that, and I see no sign of the Church in America returning to the foot of the Cross. Instead, we have continued to run away from what God is calling us to, and we have reached the edge of the cliff. Only God knows when He will allow us to fall over it.

> *I come across those who insist revival*
> *is coming.*
> *They don't want to hear about*
> *repentance and judgment,*
> *calling the message gloom and doom.*
> *Some say it to my face,*
> *others behind my back.*
> *Just like with the prophets of old.*
> *I understand.*
> *I would prefer to talk about revival.*

But it should be obvious
to anyone who has their eyes open
that an awakening is not coming
to this nation until
we lay down our idols.
And the people of the United States
will not lay down their idols until
they are forced to.
Until their backs are against
the wall.
Then they will have to make a choice.

Will you be for Christ
or against Him?

The time for sitting on the fence is over.

Now then,
if you will indeed obey My voice
and keep My covenant,
then you shall be
My own possession
among all the peoples,
for all the earth is Mine

Exodus 19:5 (NASB)

2015
A New Year

It was during the evening of January 1st. I felt so drawn just to sit in the Lord's presence. It wasn't long before He gave me a scripture in Joel.

> [14]CONSECRATE A FAST,
> PROCLAIM A SOLEMN ASSEMBLY;
> GATHER THE ELDERS
> AND ALL THE INHABITANTS OF THE LAND
> TO THE HOUSE OF THE LORD YOUR GOD.
> [15]ALAS FOR THE DAY!
> FOR THE DAY OF THE LORD IS NEAR,
> AND IT WILL COME AS DESTRUCTION FROM THE
> ALMIGHTY.
> JOEL 1:14-15 (NASB)

I continued just to sit in His presence. I didn't even feel like talking. Was this a word for 2015? I didn't know. God didn't elaborate on anything, just gave me the scripture.

Sometime later He spoke to me about obedience.

> **Obedience is key.**
> **Not partial obedience.**
> **That can still cause loss of life.**
> **Obedience.**
> **Pure.**
> **Total.**

Then later that night He gave me another scripture.

¹¹"BEHOLD, THE DAYS ARE COMING,"
DECLARES THE LORD GOD,
"WHEN I WILL SEND A FAMINE ON THE LAND,
NOT A FAMINE FOR BREAD OR A THIRST FOR WATER,
BUT RATHER FOR HEARING THE WORDS OF THE LORD."
AMOS 8:11 (NASB)

Except for giving these scriptures to me, and a personal word now and then, God was strangely quiet.

During the night of January 8th, I woke up on and off all night, praying for the people on Dauphin Island. I would go back to sleep for a while and then wake up again. Every time I woke up I knew God had put another resident from the island on my heart to pray for. I still don't know what that was about, but I don't have to. I was obedient to pray and left the rest to the Lord.

On January 15th, at 3:43am, God spoke this to me about order.

Order, My child, is a theme right now.
You will be telling many
to get things in order.
It is imperative that they do.

They must begin with their
spiritual life,
and move right on through
to every aspect.
Every single area needs to be in order.

And as they get each area
of their lives in order,
I will bless it.

The Lord didn't tell me anything else about this. Quite possibly, He thought it was self-explanatory.

I took John to the emergency room in January. We thought he might have pneumonia again. He didn't have chest pain, but was coughing a lot and really struggling to breathe.

While in the waiting room for five hours, a young couple came in. The guy was holding his head and covering his eyes. I kept watching him, waiting for a nudge from God to do something.

John said, "I bet he has a migraine."

Interesting. I had thought the same thing. Right then, I knew I was supposed to pray for him.

I had suffered with migraines for 13 years, until one night God just totally healed me. I haven't had a migraine for 18 years now. Since that time, I have felt led to pray for a number of people who have migraines.

I wasn't moving very fast to pray for this young man though. For one thing, they had moved to the other side of the room where there wasn't as much light. They also seemed very closed off. They didn't look at anybody and obviously did not want attention from anyone.

God continued to push me to pray for this young man. He wasn't just nudging anymore. As I look back on it, I'm surprised He didn't knock me right out of my chair. I was pretty consumed with what was going on with John and how sick he was. It seemed I just didn't have the strength to get up and go pray for this guy.

The couple had been in the waiting room for over an hour hour before I finally went over to pray for him. He had his entire head covered with a scarf at that point, so I asked his wife if he had a migraine. She nodded. He pulled the scarf off one eye to look at me.

I said, "God healed me of migraines 17 years ago. Would it be okay if I prayed for you?"

He took the scarf off his head and said, "Yes."

I prayed a simple prayer for his healing and went back to sit with John. As I walked back to my chair, I could not believe I had waited that long to go pray for that man. I simply asked God to forgive me.

John was immediately called back into the examining room and we were out of there in a half hour. We would probably have been out of there much earlier, had I just been obedient.

> *They gave John a breathing treatment.*
> *He didn't have pneumonia,*
> *or even bronchitis.*
> *It was the strangest thing.*
> *After we left the hospital*
> *that night,*
> *he wasn't sick anymore.*
> *And actually,*
> *hasn't been sick since then.*
>
> *Could all that have been*
> *for me to pray for that young man?*
> *Yes. I believe it could have been.*
> *I don't know if it was,*
> *But it could have been.*
> *And I felt as soon as I*
> *prayed for him,*
> *that he was healed.*
> *God will go to great lengths*
> *for just one.*
>
> *I can't help but wonder...*
> *How long God would*
> *have given me*
> *to be obedient.*
> *And if the outcome with John*
> *would have been much different,*
> *had I not been.*

Keeping Our Eyes On Jesus

I had just gone to bed. It was around 11pm on January 22nd. We were in a Walmart parking lot just south of Washington, DC. We would go into Virginia the next day.

As soon as I laid down, I felt a strong urge to write. I got back up and got out my laptop. After trying to write a chapter for this book, I realized that wasn't what the Lord wanted me to do. So I opened a new document and waited on God. It was 12:19am on January 23rd by then. The following is what the Lord gave me —

> *The world as we know it is coming to an end. It is coming to a screeching halt. Nothing, absolutely nothing, will remain the same. It will be a good different for those who are willing to totally put their trust in Me. For those who will not, that will be another story. One that does not have a happy ending. But right now I want to talk to those who WILL put their trust in ME. Totally, without thought or care of anything else.*
>
> *You will be covered under My wings. Things will look horrible out of the natural eye, but you will be seeing things through supernatural eyes. Yes, you will still see the hardship of most. You will see the pain and suffering of many. But if you look at all of this through the eyes I give you, it will enable you to help many out*

of their plight. Many will come to Me. Many will turn their hearts and lives over to Me. And many will be saved because you will see them through the eyes I give you and you will know exactly what to do, what to say, and how to help them. If you were to look at what is going on through natural eyes, you would be too distraught to be able to help anyone, including yourself! But trust is a must!

Let's look at it this way.

The shipwreck is over. People are clinging to pieces of wood, lifejackets (because most weren't even prepared enough to have put the lifejackets on), and anything else they can get their hands on. You were one of the prepared ones, one of the few who listened. You have a lifejacket on. And yet you're still bobbing about in the water, looking at the chaos all around you. People are crying for help. People are drowning, dying even as you watch. And yet you are helpless to do anything except bob in the water, watching.

Then you remember Me. You've been saying, "God help us! Save us!" But you haven't really focused on Me until now. Those words are no longer just automatically coming out of your mouth. There is now thought behind them; your heart is engaged. "God help us!" And you begin to listen. I am speaking to you. You are now seeing the shipwreck through the eyes I have given you, supernatural eyes. And you know what to do, what to say, to actually help these people and save many.

You begin to pray a salvation prayer that many will say with you, even as they go down to a watery grave, they will ascend up to Me. People will be calmed. And they will begin to be able to think more clearly, therefore helping others. Many, many lives will be saved this night because you listened to Me. I enabled you to turn the chaos around and calm the waters. All because you listened and obeyed.

There will be much chaos and confusion in the coming days. Much death and destruction. You can keep your eyes focused on what you see with your natural eyes or you can look through the eyes I give you.

The only way to see through eyes that I give you is to put all your trust in Me. There is no man, no amount of money, or anything material that will help you in the days that are getting nearer and nearer. I am your only Source. I am your only Help. Stop looking to others and other things for joy and peace. I am your only true Joy and Peace.

They lay scattered through the woods. Bodies. Death. Everywhere. The vultures were swooping down upon them. If only they had listened. If only they had put their trust in the One who deserves their trust. They would have made it to a safe place. If only they had taken the road I tried to direct them to. But the crowd was going this way...

They didn't prepare. Didn't spend time talking with Me, so they didn't even recognize My voice as I tried to get them on the right path.

> *Before you ask,*
> *yes, the Lord told me all this.*
> *Many of you are thinking*
> *how horrible it all sounds.*
> *But a few of you were*
> *really "listening" as you read.*
> *You hear the hope amid the chaos.*
> *You hear the calm in the storm.*
> *You hear the promises of the Lord.*
>
> *And what is He saying?*
> *We are to keep our eyes on Him.*
> *We are to trust Him absolutely.*
> *He will protect and keep us.*
> *And He will use us to rescue others.*

Yes.
Hope abounds in this story
from the Lord.
I believe it sounds a little
like a parable.
How about you?

God has been speaking to me during this entire journey about the importance of keeping our eyes on Him. While that is something we should have been doing during our entire walk with Him, it is especially important in the season we are living in.

I believe we are going to see things that will cause us to just give up, sights that will even make some want to take their own lives. We simply must not take in what is going on without filtering it through the Holy Spirit. If we keep our eyes on the Lord, I believe He will give us the wisdom and discernment needed to process what we are seeing and therefore be used of God for His purposes.

In 2 Kings chapter 2, we read about Elijah being taken up to heaven. In verse 9, Elijah asks Elisha, "What can I do for you before I am taken up?"

Elisha answers, "Let a double portion of thy spirit be upon me."

Elijah responds, "You have asked a hard thing: nevertheless, if you see me when I am taken from you, you will receive what you have asked for, but if not, it shall not be so."

In verse 11 we find, as they walked on, and talked, a chariot of fire and horses of fire appeared and separated them...and Elijah went up by a whirlwind into heaven.

And Elisha saw it...

And he received his double portion.

Had Elisha taken his eyes off his master even for a moment, he would have missed it. But even through the chariots of fire, and being parted from his master by the horses of fire, Elisha never allowed his gaze to be distracted from Elijah.

We cannot allow ourselves to be distracted by *anything* that is going on around us!

We must keep our eyes on our Master. The Ruler of the wind and seas, Maker of heaven and earth. Our Savior, Redeemer and Friend. The Author and Finisher of our faith.

He is the One to watch...always.

For if you confess with your mouth
that Jesus is Lord
and believe in your heart
that God raised him from the dead,
you will be saved.

Romans 10:9 (NLT)

Be Faithful

It was just after midnight on February 16th, 2015, when the Lord told me I needed to make note of today's date. He said I had two months to meet with the people who were on my heart and share the words He had given me.

I didn't waste any time. Two months is a very short time to meet with all those who were on my heart.

It was also during this time when the Lord told me I needed to schedule a few meetings in conference rooms. I knew those rooms would be expensive. I had never paid for a place to hold a meeting. But I knew God had a purpose for what He was asking me to do, so for every location I spoke, at least one meeting was held in a conference room. I believe people came to those meetings who simply wouldn't have come had the meeting been in a church or someone's home. Those rooms were very neutral ground. Our team would go in to pray and anoint the room before the meeting began, and the presence of the Lord was always evident.

An interesting thing happened each and every time I was going into an area and needed a conference room. Someone offered to pay for the room immediately! It was almost as though that person had been just waiting to take care of the cost of that particular room. We really saw God at work in this and the confirmation was so encouraging.

The messages for these meetings were similar to what they had been in the past, but God had added something new. He began to speak to me about miracles.

The scripture God kept giving me was 2 Kings 4 and 5. God continued to show me that we always have a part to play in receiving our miracle.

As you read those two chapters you'll find, in every single case, each person who received a miracle had to do their part.

In Chapter 4, we find the widow who was just about to lose her two sons to the creditors. She spoke to Elisha and he asked her what she had in her house. She didn't have anything except a pot of oil. So Elisha told her to go to all her neighbors and borrow pots and jars. He told her to get a lot of them. Then to go into her house, shut the door, and pour the oil she had into those vessels. She was obedient to do exactly that. And she received her miracle! Her oil didn't run out until she had filled every single container she had borrowed. Then Elisha told her to sell what she needed to pay the creditors, and she would have enough left over for her and her sons to live on.

In Chapter 5, we find Naaman, the leper, who goes to see the prophet, Elisha, after his wife's maid says he would be healed if he went to see him.

Elisha told Naaman to go wash in the Jordan River seven times and he would be healed. Naaman was not happy! He wanted the prophet to do something more extraordinary. But Naaman's servant told him he should at least try it. So he dipped himself seven times in the Jordan River and was healed.

There are other miracles in these two chapters, but I will leave you to read those for yourself. The point is, these people had to do their part in order to receive the miracle God had for them. I believe you will find that is the case in almost every miracle recorded in the Bible.

The same holds true for today. We have a part to play in receiving our miracle. It may be as simple as getting out of your seat and walking down to the altar, or asking someone to pray for you. It could even be simply believing God will heal you. But God could ask you to do something a little more in order to receive your miracle.

God wants to partner with us in everything. Yes, God is the One who performs the miraculous, but He wants us to be a part of it, not just a bystander. Although, sometimes those bystanders are recipients of miracles, as well. I know from my own experience, once you have truly received a miracle from the Lord, you will no longer be a bystander. You will want to be part of what He is doing.

I used those two months to share all the words God had put on my heart with all the people who were on my heart. It was a time of almost back-to-back meetings, some large, some small, but all of them were fruitful. It was a time of ministering to, and sharing with, people who are dear to me. In every meeting, I looked out over the faces of those who have been so faithful anytime I have been in their area, to attend every meeting they possibly could, to support us financially, pray for us, encourage us, and love on us. There is no way I could put into words how much they mean to us. No matter what lies up ahead, I know the Lord will cover these people, as they have covered us.

I still do not totally understand the two-month time frame, but I have come to a place where I don't have to understand. I only have to be obedient. The rest I leave in God's hands.

The Lord spoke to me about this near the end of that two-month time frame.

> I know those people are dear
> to your heart.
> They have been faithful
> to hear the word of the Lord
> as you have been faithful
> to carry it to them.
>
> You must be faithful
> to those who have been faithful.

This was all the confirmation I needed.

Around that same time, God gave this word to me.

Do not grow weary.
Those who have been obedient.
Those who have listened to the call.
Do not grow weary.
You will see the fruit of your labors.

Continue the walk, my friend,
to which God has called you.
The road may have bumps
and even boulders,
but God is faithful
to get you through.
It is hard sometimes...
believe me, I know.
But I also know...
You can all do hard things.

For with God,
nothing is impossible.

Suddenly

I need to share a dream with you. I woke up from this dream in the early morning hours of April 11th. Read this carefully. Maybe more than once. I believe this dream is very important and the Lord wants to speak to each one of you about it.

I was walking, walking, walking...through beautiful fields. It was a gorgeous sunny day. I kept looking up at the blue sky with just a small, puffy, white cloud here and there. The trees were so tall and green. A gentle breeze barely blowing in the tops of them. The grass was thick and green with a few flowers scattered through the fields.

While I appreciated all the beauty, I couldn't seem to take it in as I normally do. I kept looking back at the people who were following me.

They were farther back than I would have liked them to be. I wasn't really comfortable with them being so far behind me. They sure weren't showing any signs of getting closer either. If anything, they kept dropping farther and farther back.

They were scattered out across the field, laughing, talking, pushing each other around a little in fun. Just all around having a great time. Normally, I would have been in the middle of all that, but I knew these weren't normal times. I sensed an urgency that none of them seemed to understand.

I kept stopping to turn around and call back to them. Trying to get them to hurry, to catch up with me, but it was to no avail. Finally, I sat down on a rock to wait. I knew I couldn't wait for long. And soon I was up again, waving for them to come on, calling to them...calling to them.

The next time I turned around, they were farther back still. And then farther, and farther.

I continued on. I knew I must.

All of a sudden I looked down at my feet, and I was standing in ash. As far as I could see, there was nothing except what looked like ashes on the ground. The trees that had been so beautiful a moment before were either gone or looked like they had been through a fire with just a few broken, charred branches left behind.

I turned slowly to look behind me. Afraid of what I might find. I didn't see any of those who had been behind me. There was no sign of life anywhere.

But I knew I must continue on.

I have intentionally
not shared anything
I sensed or felt
about this dream
in the book.
I believe you all
need to ask God,
"What does this mean for me?"

I shared this dream
the following day
with a group of people.
Two people in that group
shared with me that
they had had a dream
very similar to mine.
One was the same night
and the other was
the night before my dream.

God is showing us something here.

On Assignment

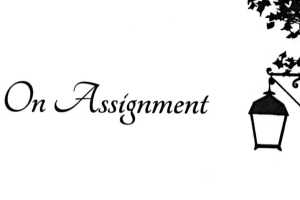

It was Saturday afternoon. John and I were driving across Interstate 40 on our way to Knoxville. We were in the mountains of North Carolina, just west of Asheville. We heard something and John said, "I have to pull over!" The noise didn't sound that loud to me, but he had obviously heard something in it that I hadn't. So he pulled off to the shoulder right away.

The traffic was horrendous! We couldn't get very far off the road. Thankfully, the problem seemed to be on the passenger side. The panel over the dual tires in back was just barely hanging on. John tried to look under it and at the tires, but couldn't see much. He got some plastic ties and re-attached the panel. We got back on the highway and began to smell rubber very quickly. John got off at Exit 24, just four miles from where we had pulled off the road. There was a Pilot station so we pulled in. John suspected a blowout but he had been unable to check it out good because of the traffic. Sure enough, he found that the inside tire had a split in the side of it.

Well, it could be much worse, we thought. How hard could it be for our roadside assistance to bring out a tire and put it on? I called them only to find out it was going to cost us almost $1000 for them to bring a tire and put it on the motor home! I couldn't believe it! I got off the phone and began to call other places in the area. Most were closed and the people I spoke with were very nice but didn't have a tire to match what we had.

After about three hours of trying to find someone to bring us a tire, I felt we should just find a campground close by and try to get there for the weekend. Thank goodness the Smoky Mountains is full of campgrounds!

We had been praying on and off during this entire process, and now John and I prayed for the exact campground God wanted us to go to. I checked our campground book and found one five miles away. After calling them to make sure they had a spot available, we decided that's where we should go. We were able to stay for half price with our membership card and the lady said they were closing the office, but we could choose a spot and settle up in the morning.

John talked to a truck driver about driving on the tire and he told him it would be fine if we went slow and didn't let the tire get hot.

Sure enough, it was exactly five miles and we had no trouble getting there. Normally, we try to find a campsite that isn't right next to other campers if we can, but I was so tired I just told John to pull into almost the first open one we came to. He got out to hook everything up and I began the job of getting things ready inside. I could hear the couple that we saw sitting at the picnic table at the site next to us talking to John. They sounded really friendly. I usually enjoy that, but today I was hot, tired, frustrated, and irritable! I didn't want to get out and chit-chat with anyone. But God was urging me to go talk to them, so out I went.

John had already told them we were in full time ministry on the road and the lady began to ask about that. I could tell she knew about things of the Lord by the way she spoke. She introduced herself as Sharon, and then introduced Andrew, very nice people. As we continued to talk, she shared a lot about her walk with the Lord. She had been involved in ministry in the past, but had gotten away from church. After moving to another state, she had been unable to find the right church and wasn't currently attending anywhere.

As I stood there listening to her, the Holy Spirit began to speak to me about the man.

God spoke to me clearly, "Ask him if he knows Jesus as his Savior."

So I did.

He didn't seem real uncomfortable but, as he hesitated, I could tell he didn't know the Lord. Finally, he told me he wasn't sure what that meant but that he didn't think so. I explained it to him. He had a bit of a hard time with the fact that it was so simple to accept the Lord. He told me his mother had become a born-again Christian a few years ago, and that she had been talking to him and praying for him a lot since then. His girlfriend, the lady who was with him, had also been talking to him.

Then Andrew said, "I need to write this stuff down about how to ask Jesus into my heart, because I won't remember all of it."

God spoke to me again. "Ask him if he wants to pray right now."

So I told him it was fine to write it down, but would he like to pray right now to accept the Lord?

"Yes," he answered me immediately. "Yes, but I don't know what to say."

I told him I would pray and then he could just pray after me, repeating the words I said, if he liked. He did.

Within 30 minutes after John and I got to that campground, Andrew had accepted the Lord! I was blown away! What a God set-up! Even Andrew and his girlfriend recognized it.

He said, "God sent you here, didn't He?"

"Yes, He did," I replied.

I took a Bible over to him a little later. A nice men's devotional Bible, two-toned brown leather. He was thrilled with it. He asked me if he should just start at the beginning and I told him maybe he could begin with the New Testament. He gave me $20 and said it was all the cash he had. I didn't want to take it, but I could tell he wanted to do something for me. He said there was no way he could repay me for what I had done for him. But it's really what Jesus did, not me. I was just on assignment, doing what God had led me to do.

Then he told me he felt different.

"Am I supposed to feel different already?" he asked.

I just smiled at him. There was no need to answer. He had more questions. Good questions. And I answered them as well as I could.

Finally, I got ready to leave, reminding Andrew to call his Mom.

The next morning, they could hardly wait to talk to me. I went over and Andrew had a story to tell me about calling his mom.

She had been at a ladies' meeting on Saturday morning. The speaker had told them to get out a pencil and paper and write down the #1 thing they wanted God to do for them.

And she had written down "Save my son."

She told Andrew she hadn't expected it this quick!

Andrew also told me he was going to keep his promise to read something in his Bible every day. He had read the first chapter of Matthew. My heart was so warmed by all I was hearing.

So Saturday morning a mother had asked God to save her son. By 1pm John and I had a blowout, couldn't find a tire and, by being sensitive to the Holy Spirit, had ended up at the campground right next to where Andrew was parked.

Through being sensitive to the Holy Spirit, AND being obedient, even in a situation where I didn't necessarily feel like it, Andrew had come into the Kingdom of God.

Thank You, Lord. Thank You for saving Andrew and for allowing me to be a part of Your mighty plan. Help me to remember that I am "On Assignment" always and at all times.

I absolutely believe
God allowed us
to have that tire blowout
in order to get us
right where He wanted us.

He heard that mother's plea
for her son to be saved,
and He set it in motion.

We must understand that
all who call themselves
Christians
are in the Army of God.

And those who are
totally sold out to Him
are in the Elite Forces.
We must live our
entire lives
"On Assignment."

If my people,
which are called by my name,
shall humble themselves,
and pray,
and seek
my face,
and turn from
their wicked ways;
then will I hear
from heaven,
and will forgive their sin,
and will
heal their land.

2 Chronicles 7:14 (KJV)

Hickory, North Carolina

Around this time, God began to speak to me about having a meeting in Hickory. Although we had lived in Hickory, North Carolina, for almost twenty years before going on the road in full-time ministry, the Lord had only led me to speak in that area a couple of times.

He told me the meeting was to be held in June at a conference center and even showed me which one. As always, God provided someone to take care of the cost.

As I began the preparation for this meeting, the Lord began to speak to me about having two meetings. One would be to talk about our walk of faith and the beginning of the journey, the other would be to share more recent words from the Lord. I was a little hesitant about two meetings.

"What if people don't come," I thought. "Or if they only come to one meeting and the other one is almost empty."

God spoke to me clearly about that.

> **Are you really going to limit Me like that?**

"No, God. I'm not. I will schedule two meetings and leave the rest up to You."

The conference in Hickory was definitely a success by human standards.

Both meetings were well attended and those present appeared attentive and receptive to what the Lord was saying. I am still receiving positive and encouraging emails and text messages that lead back to that conference.

I have learned not to calculate anything by standards other than the Lord's. I try to view success from His measuring stick. Numbers aren't important. Two people who are truly listening and have a heart to be obedient will accomplish more than 200 mediocre Christians.

Are the people listening? Are they receiving the words from Him? Will they spend more time with the Lord, asking Him what He would have them to do with what they have heard at these meetings? And then, are they going to be obedient to do what God is asking them to?

I believe those things are at least part of what God would consider a successful meeting. And I believe the Hickory conference was a success in God's eyes, as well.

I want to leave you with just a few things the people heard there.

In early May, God gave me this word.

You have until the end of the summer.

I began to pray about this. I knew it wasn't just a personal word for me, but one that I was to share with as many people as possible.

As I continued to pray over the next few days, He revealed to me more about what this word meant.

By the end of the summer, we all need to have taken care of everything God has put on our hearts. We need to stop procrastinating and DO all that He has told us to do!

God wasn't telling me disaster would strike at the end of the summer. Although I knew it could. He was saying we all need to take care of the things He has told us to. Many of us need a deadline in order to get things done.

It might be as simple as doing something kind for your neighbor, and it could be as huge as what God has called my husband and I to do. Most of you will fall somewhere in the middle.

Repentance, preparation for the days ahead, and drawing closer to the Lord are for everyone, and those things are definitely at the top of the list.

In the early morning hours on the day of the conference, I was awakened by the Lord. He gave me this word for Hickory, North Carolina.

Word from the Lord for Hickory, North Carolina
Released June 13th, 2015

> **I want to use this place as a city of refuge.**
> **That's why I've sent My servant.**
> **But things must be done first.**
>
> **Hearts must be cleansed.**
>
> **There is sin in the camp of My people.**
>
> **They need to get their priorities straight.**
>
> **It's NOT all about you. Get your eyes off of yourself**
> **and focus on Me – Almighty God.**
> **Then we will move forward.**
>
> **I sent My servant here more than 20 years ago –**
> **for a time, such as this.**

Listen. Listen.
Stop wasting time fighting amongst yourselves and
get on your knees.
Get your own heart clean.
The rest will take care of itself.
I will see to that.

There isn't much time.
Stop wasting it!

Then God gave me this scripture.

> [11]BUT MY PEOPLE DID NOT LISTEN TO MY VOICE,
> AND ISRAEL DID NOT OBEY ME.
> [12]SO I GAVE THEM OVER TO THE STUBBORNNESS OF
> THEIR HEART, TO WALK IN THEIR OWN DEVICES.
> [13]OH, THAT MY PEOPLE WOULD LISTEN TO ME,
> THAT ISRAEL WOULD WALK IN MY WAYS!
> [14]I WOULD QUICKLY SUBDUE THEIR ENEMIES
> AND TURN MY HAND AGAINST THEIR ADVERSARIES.
> [15]THOSE WHO HATE THE LORD WOULD PRETEND
> OBEDIENCE TO HIM, AND THEIR TIME OF PUNISHMENT
> WOULD BE FOREVER.
> [16]BUT I WOULD FEED YOU WITH THE FINEST OF THE
> WHEAT,
> AND WITH HONEY FROM THE ROCK I WOULD SATISFY
> YOU.
>
> PSALM 81:11-16 (NASB)

Listed below are three of the things God gave me as I was preparing for those meetings.

1. **Salvation – for yourself and others**
   Do you know you have received salvation?
   Is there someone God has put on your heart
   to talk to about salvation?
   Take care of these things immediately!
   Do not delay!

2. **Get right with God**
   While these things seem obvious to some of us,
   there are many who call themselves Christians,

pastors even, who are holding onto their little pet sins, or their big pet sins. Is there something you have given so much time and attention to that God has been pushed into 2nd place, or even 3rd or 4th place in your life? Search your heart. Ask God to show you if there is anything you need to repent for and put in its proper place in your life or get rid of altogether.

3. **Are you being obedient with your money?**
What is God telling you to do in this area?
If you don't know, ask Him. Then be obedient.
More and more people are being led to sell things in order to get out of debt and live a simpler life. I'm not saying that's what God is telling you. I just want you to talk to Him about it. And then make certain you are willing to do what He is asking you to.

God is trying to get us prepared for the storm that is coming. For the destruction that is imminent in this country. I do not know what any of that will look like. I only know for certain that the remnant who listens to the Lord, and is obedient to His voice, will have a much easier time than those who refuse to listen.

I hear Christians frequently saying we are going to be raptured out of here before we experience hardship. What I am speaking about is not the return of Jesus. Jesus will return, that much is certain. I do not know when that will be. What I am referring to is judgment on America because we, as a nation, have turned away from God.

Others talk about a revival that is going to sweep the land and change everything. Yes. There will be an awakening in our country, but it will not happen until we see much devastation. People in the United States of America are going to have to get extremely desperate before they will admit they have sinned and turn back to God.

Then there are those who are putting their trust in a new political administration. They believe that will turn this country around.

Friends, please understand, our nation is too far gone for that! The only One who can help us is Almighty God.

Anyone who considers that the United States may escape judgment has not taken into consideration what we must look like to God about now.

I know there are those who truly love the Lord, those who read their Bible and try to live by it. But how many Christians are still trying to ride the fence? They just want enough of God to get by, not enough to take them out of their comfort zone.

Get into the Word of God and read for yourself what God considers an abomination. You don't need me to spell this out for you. And what about our idols in this country? As a nation, we have placed so many things before God that He is near the bottom of the list.

The United States of America has been the most blessed nation on earth! And what have we done with those blessings?

You may say, I haven't done these things! And maybe you haven't. But do you go to church? If so, you have to take some responsibility for what goes on in your church. Do you call yourself an American? Are you a citizen of this nation? Then stand up and take some responsibility! Anything you are a part of, you have some responsibility for.

Our liberties and freedoms are being snatched out of our hands one by one. Don't just sit back and expect someone else to do your part. Our religious freedom is not just slipping away, it is like a snowball rolling downhill, gathering speed as it goes. If we do not stand together for our freedoms, it will not be long before those freedoms are a thing of the past.

Get before the Lord and ask Him what He would have you to do, and then just do it.

He Will...
if
We Will

I know you have read many difficult things in this book. But please remember – God only brings judgment because He wants people to turn back to Him. He loves us all so much that He will do whatever it takes to turn the hearts of people to His Son, Jesus Christ.

Everywhere I have gone in the past few months, people are feeling the urgency of what's coming and are concerned they haven't done enough to prepare. They are feeling the burden of needing to "do more."

If this is you, I want you to know that, if you are being obedient to the best of your ability to do what God has told you to do, then rest in that. God is looking at your heart, not your pantry. This does not mean we should just sit back and wait for God to provide. I believe He expects each of us to do our part, and we can always count on Him to be faithful to help us.

If after searching your heart, you believe you have been negligent in doing what you should have done, then simply repent and ask God to help you. It is never too late to begin a walk of obedience to the Lord.

We are going to see God do amazing miracles during the season we are living in. Do not be afraid to ask Him for what you and others have need of.

Remember – He will...if we will.

I don't know about you
but I do not look forward
to my children and grandchildren
living in a country
that has fallen
to the depths this nation
has fallen to.

Is God finished with America?
No!
I do not believe God
is finished with America!
If He was, there would be
no judgment.
God brings judgment
to turn nations around.
And the United States desperately
needs to turn around.

I say to Almighty God, our Father,
the Maker of heaven and earth,
"Your will be done, Lord.
We are Yours.
We claim this nation for You.
Do with us as You will."

How many will stand with me?

Words from the Lord

The Lord has revealed to me that it will be extremely important in the days to come for all of us to remember, and to be able to recall with clarity, the words He has given us—words of repentance, warning, preparation, judgment, trust, and hope.

This section contains a collection of many important words from the Lord, and will enable the readers to quickly locate them as the need arises. You will find these words within the chapters of the book as well. They are listed chronologically from 2007 through 2015.

God clearly showed me this section of the book and the importance of listing the words here. As we see things approaching, a quick look in the back of this book will remind us that none of this is any surprise to Him. God is still in control and remains on the throne. We will also see His references as to what we, His people, need to do.

May you stay under His wings.

Still Following the Call,

November 14th, 2007

Life as we know it is about to change.
If there is anything you need to repent of,
anything at all between you and God,
you need to take care of it.
And call your congregation to do the same.

April 8th, 2009

I am looking for a remnant.
A remnant who will repent.
First of all, to cleanse their own hearts and
then, to cleanse their nation.
Make no mistake, judgment is still coming,
but it will not be nearly as severe if I can find a
remnant who will repent for the sins of their nation.
This nation must turn and turn quickly
if there is to be any hope for survival.

June 2011

I want all the pastors in the city
to clear their schedules once a week,
to meet together and pray for their nation,
their city, and their state, in that order.
They must come into this with
clean hands and a clean heart.

January 12th, 2012

**I want them to step up to My throne.
To come boldly to the throne of grace
and cry out for mercy for their nation.**

April 2012

There is a huge storm coming to this nation.
Not necessarily a physical storm,
but a storm nonetheless.

May 3rd, 2012

I have a message for you.
Hard times are coming.
Prepare, prepare, prepare.

If they are not prepared,
many won't make it.

Many will lose everything,
but they can save their lives
and their families
if they will only listen.

Prepare, My child.
They must prepare.
Even the animals prepare
for the seasons.

It's a requirement, My child.
not a suggestion.

They must prepare in the Word
and in their relationship with Me.

Study, memorize, spend time with Me.

Learn to hear My voice clearer
than the person closest to you.

Prepare.

Those who aren't prepared
won't make it.

Get your mind off things that
have no eternal value.

Stop spending money unnecessarily.
Simply stop.

Stop running to and fro as though
you don't know what you're doing.

Prioritize your time and
spend most of it with Me.

You may think you're prepared.
Think again.

June 25th, 2012

> Those who have prepared out of a
> wrong heart will not be using
> what they have stored up.
>
> The righteous will get it.
> I will see that the righteous get it.

August 6th, 2012

I want all believers off Facebook.

My child, Facebook is an addiction.
And it's doing more harm than
drugs and alcohol combined,
because it's accepted, it's legal,
and it's free.

Marriages are falling apart
and children are being neglected
and even abused.

Countless, countless hours
are being stolen from Me.

There will come a time when
all those people would give
anything to have that time back,
but of course it is gone –
forever.

Tell this everywhere you go,
My child.

You will not be popular for it,
but I will cause conviction to rise up

in the hearts of people,
and many will turn back to Me
and break away.

They are tracking Christians
even now, on Facebook.

It will be a huge tool for the enemy
when the persecution moves in.

September 6th, 2012

There is a deceiving spirit closing
in on your nation, My child,
threatening to suffocate
each and every one.

My children *must, must* move
closer to Me every day,
must keep moving forward
if they are to be free of this
deceiving spirit.
It is a very powerful spirit,
My child.

It will suck everyone in
who is not pressing in to Me.

Stay covered.
Stay close.

October 29, 2012
A Word for New Mexico

> If they will pray in earnest,
> repent for their state and their nation,
> and ask Me to cover their state, I will.
> I will protect them.
> But they must come to Me with
> clean hands, and a clean, sincere heart.

November 9th, 2012

Just as you hear the wind blowing, My child,
My Holy Spirit is doing a work
in the hearts of people.
But it will not become apparent
until there is much
persecution and destruction.

Then you will see manifestations
of My glory as never before.

November 10th, 2012

You are to give a word, My child.
A word in Arizona.
That is why you're here.

The storm is coming!
Prepare your people.
Prepare now!

They must draw near to Me
or they will not be protected
in the days to come.

And you will be held accountable
if you do not help your people
prepare for what is coming.

Fast, pray, and prepare.

November 11th, 2012

You have been very discouraged,
distraught even,
over the results of the election.

If you need to grieve over it,
do so, but make it brief.

There is much work to be done
and not much time to do it.

Our job as people of God hasn't changed!

And no matter who sits
in the White House,
God is still on the throne!

December 1st, 2012

One thing people need to hear is this,
My child.

When they have no hope,
they can turn to Me.

When all hope is gone,
when all the things in and of
this world hold nothing for them,
they can turn to Me.

They can turn to Me.
And I will be there
with open arms to receive them.

February 15th, 2013

My child, I will speak to you now.
Listen and write.

Many children will suffer because
their parents wouldn't listen.

Wives will suffer because their
husbands wouldn't listen.

Just as the Israelites didn't like
the change in their lives when
they were brought out of Egypt,
and so they rebelled,
the same will happen here in America.

Many will not listen.
Many will rebel.

But I still have a remnant.
It is small, but growing.

And they are listening.
They are not going to rebel
when times get tough
and their comforts are taken away.

They are going to move with Me.
They are going to stay under My shelter.
And they will be My harvesters
when the time is ready.

March 16th, 2013
A word initially given in Chicago, Illinois

Stand. You must learn to stand.

There will be much persecution,
especially in this area.

If you have prepared in your heart
ahead of time, it will be much
easier to take a firm stand for Christ
when the time comes.

Are you ready to stand?

June 16th, 2013
(Originally given to me October 26th, 2008)

My people are going about in their
usual manner.
The Church is still interested in
meetings and programs.
If ever there was a time for
sackcloth and ashes, it is now.

Your country is in deep trouble,
My child.
Many people recognize it,
believers and unbelievers alike.
The difference is, the believers
should know what to do about it,
but there are very few on their
faces to Me.

Now is the time for crying out to God,
for fasting, for sacrifice.
Judgment is at hand!

If you could see ahead,
you would shake with fear.
But there is no need to fear.
I will take care of My own.

I will hide them under My wings
until the calamity has passed.
But they need to be in prayer,
repenting, fasting, crying out
for mercy and for the
judgment to be lessened.

The time is now!
Don't wait until it is too late!

August 1st, 2013

You are to tell the ladies this,
My child.

Get your house in order.
Each one will know what this
means to them.

Get your house in order and do
it quickly.
Do not lag.
This is for your own protection
and that of your family.

Get your house in order!
The time is short!
Do not act as if you have forever
to do it.

The time is short, My child,
and they will regret it if they
do not pay heed to this warning.

January 11th, 2014

You must listen carefully.
I am giving you a new word of great importance.
One people haven't heard from you before.

Listen, My child.
Get it down carefully.

People must be thankful. Thankful. Thankful.
It must be their new way of life.

If they want to hold on to what they are thankful for,
they must begin to speak it out.
Cry it out to Me.
I want to hear of their thankfulness.

I want to hear a cry of thankfulness shout up
from the earth as never before in history!
I want to hear it loud and clear.
Every day! Everywhere! From everyone!
I must hear it! As a chorus!
They must speak it out.
It needs to be the subject of the day. Every day.

Let's not talk about what's coming.
Let's talk about your thankfulness.
Write it! Speak it! Shout it! Yes!!

Thankfulness will fill the skies.

The enemy will be thwarted, confused, and confounded!

Let it begin!

August 19th, 2014

The heavens are going to break
forth with rain.
My rain.
It will be a cleansing rain,
a purifying rain.
It will equip and prepare
those who need strengthened
for the days ahead.

It will fall everywhere.
Absolutely everywhere.
People must only be open
to receive it.

Look to the heavens
with arms open wide
and breathe in my rain.

It will strengthen you,
free you, and prepare you
for what you must walk through
in the days to come.
And these days will be soon.
Do not be deceived.

September 16th, 2014

Tell them this country is under
judgment and severe persecution
is coming.

Tell them they need to make certain
they can stand when the time comes-
and it will come - especially for pastors.

They need not fear to take a stand
for Me because I will take care of
My own.

These pastors have been hand-picked,
chosen by Me, for such a time as this.
I will provide all they need
to do what I have called them to do.
But they must do it My way.
relinquish the reins to Me.
And I will guide them every step
of the way.

It's coming quickly.
It's coming fast.
Be ready.

Do not be caught with your hands
on the reins.
Allow Me to do the leading.

June 13th, 2015
Word from the Lord for Hickory, North Carolina

I want to use this place as a city of refuge.
That's why I've sent My servant.
But things must be done first.

Hearts must be cleansed.

There is sin in the camp of My people.

They need to get their priorities straight.
It's NOT all about you. Get your eyes off of yourself
and focus on Me - Almighty God.
Then we will move forward.

I sent My servant here more than 20 years ago -
for a time such as this.

Listen. Listen.
Stop wasting time fighting amongst yourselves
and get on your knees.
Get your own heart clean.
The rest will take care of itself.
I will see to that.

There isn't much time.
Stop wasting it!

October 5th, 2015
Word from the Lord for Columbia, South Carolina, after the flood of 2015

What if that hurricane would have hit full on?

There needs to be praise instead of sorrow.
I have saved them!
I have spared them!

No! This is not a trial run!
This is My hand of mercy.
This is My protection.

Wake up! Wake up!

Look what it could have been?

And praise Me for My hand of protection on this area.
I have cupped you in My hand as the water rushed in.

Draw near. Draw near. In Thanksgiving and Praise!

Use this as a time to gather in the harvest.

And listen. Listen for My voice.
This is only the beginning of what is to come
upon this land.

Keep your eyes on Me.

Use this as a time to draw others into the Kingdom.
You must not waste a moment.
A moment could be a soul.

Praise Me! Praise Me! Quickly and sincerely!

I have cupped you in the palm of My hand.

August 19th, 2015
Word from the Lord for Dauphin Island, Alabama

I have a word for you to give these precious people
on the island.

Life has been hard here. For some, very hard.
And I want to warn you – difficult days are ahead.
But take heart, they will not last forever!

And remember, always remember –
I have not forgotten you.

This island will be set apart as a special place to
be used by Me.
But you must! You simply MUST keep your eyes on Me,
remember that I love you,
and I have not forgotten you are out here on this island.
Because for a time it may feel that way.

But My hand is on this island in a special way.
It is a set apart place.
I will use the island mightily.

Do not fear the dark and difficult days ahead.
I have a plan and a purpose,
and I will use those who remain on this island
to carry it out.

But if you are not prepared to "ride out the storm" –
Pack up and get off the island.

For those who are willing to trust Me –
Keep your eyes on Me,
not on what is going on around you.

And remember – I will NEVER forget you!
And I am faithful in all situations.

I love you. With all My heart.

Psalm 17
Meditate on that.

And remember that I have not forgotten you
here on this island.

You are set apart to do My work here.

Continue to prepare for it.

CPSIA information can be obtained
at www.ICGtesting.com
Printed in the USA
FFOW01n1245230116
20710FF